CSS and HTML for beginners

A Beginners HTML and CSS Guide to Developing a Strong Coding Foundation, Building Responsive Website and Creating Standard Web page

By

Ethan Hall

HTML+CSS

Design and Build Web Sites

JON DUCKETT

trademarks and brands within this book are for clarifying purposes only and are owned by the owner, not affiliated with this document.

Table of Contents

HTML FOR BEGINNERS

CSS FOR BEGINNERS

HTML

For Beginners

A Complete Beginners HTML Guide to Developing a Strong Coding Foundation and Mastering the Fundamentals of Modern Web Design

By

Ethan Hall

Introduction

You adore the Web, and if you've read this far, you do as well. Around the same time, the Internet is complex, noisy, thrilling, interesting, and useful. From a user's perspective, the Internet is a lot of fun, but that's just half of the picture. The Internet's participatory nature is maybe its strongest feature. You can create your material — a tree! It's incredible. There has never been a contact system like this. Anyone with a basic PC and a little experience will start their home-stead over one of the most thrilling networks in the development of communication.

The main issue is figuring out what to do. Often website development books are just about learning how to use apps that you have to purchase. That's well, but it's not needed. Many software programs have emerged to render web creation simpler — and some of them perform very well — but regardless of the software product you use, you also need to understand what's going on beneath the surface. It is where this book enters the image.

This book would teach you everything you need to know about the Internet. You'll learn how to use various apps, but most importantly, you'll build your web page.

You'll find out:

You'll learn how websites are made and the fundamental layout of web pages. Since you create your pages, you'll have a good understanding of the structure. There are no enigmas online.

What is the difference between substance and style? You'll grasp the fundamental tenet of contemporary Internet thinking: that style and substance can be kept apart.

How to use network standards: The Internet is a jumbled mess, but out of the chaos, several standards have emerged. You'll learn how these standards function and how to put them to use.

How to make attractive web pages: By default, you want the website to look great. You'll learn how to use shape, pattern, color, and photographs in this book.

How to create modern layouts: Several websites have tables, lists, and other fancy elements. You'll work out where to build it.

Add Interactive elements: The other languages enable you to add forms to your websites, validate form details, and create animations.

Chapter-1 Overview of HTML

Tim Berners-Lee, a scientist at the CERN science institute in Switzerland, coined HTML. He introduced the concept of a hypertext structure built on the Internet. HTML is abbreviated as Hypertext Markup Language. It helps the user build and structure lines, chapters, headings, connections, and blockquotes for websites and applications.

HTML isn't a programming language, so it can't do anything like build complex functionality. Instead, it allows you to arrange and type papers in the same way as Microsoft Word does.

The most commonly used language for writing Web pages is HTML. The way Websites (HTML documents) are connected referred to as Hypertext. As a result, the relation accessible on a website is referred to as Hypertext.

HTML stands for Hypertext Markup Language, which means you can use it to "markup" textual content with tags that inform a Web viewer how to view it. HTML was created to describe the layout of documents such as headings, paragraphs, indexes, and so on to make scientific knowledge more easily shared amongst researchers. HTML is also commonly used to structure web pages using the various tags included in the HTML language, such as <article>, <header>, and <footer>.

1.1 How Does HTML Work?

HTML archives are files with the extensions.html and.htm. Any web browser can be used to use them (such as Safari, Mozilla Firefox or Google Chrome). The HTML file is interpreted by the browser, which renders the material for internet users to see. Typically, a website would have many separate HTML sections. About pages, email pages and Home pages for example, will have their own HTML records. Each HTML page is made up of a series of tags (also known as elements), which can be thought of as the web page's building blocks. They organize the material into pages, headings, chapters, and other content blocks using a hierarchy. The <tag> </tag> syntax is used for the opening and closing of most HTML objects. Here's an illustration of how HTML components should be organized in code:

```
<div>
<h2>The Heading</h2>
<h3>Sun heading</h3>
<p>One Paragraph</p>
<img src="/" alt="picture">
<p>It is paragraph-2 <a href="https://google.com">hyper_link</a></p>
</div>
```

The final aspect is a basic division (div>/div>) that can be used to separate larger material pieces. A heading (h1>/h1>), a subheading (h2>/h2>), two paragraphs (p>/p>), and a graphic (img>) are all included. A connect (a>/a>) with a href element that contains the target URL is used in the second paragraph. There are two other attributes on the image tag: src for the picture direction and alt and picture definition.

1.2 Most Used HTML Tags

H inline tags and Block-level are the two kinds of HTML tags. Block-level components take up the entire usable room in the document and often launch a new line. Block tags are often seen in headings and paragraphs. Inline components just take as much room as they require and do not break the page's flow. They're used to format the inside contents of block-level objects. Inline tags include things like links and highlighted strings. HTML's Advantages and Disadvantages HTML, like other products, has its own set of advantages and disadvantages.

Advantages:

A commonly spoken language with a large population and a wealth of capital. Every web browser supports it natively. It has a simple learning curve. It's fully free and open-source.

Markup that is neat and reliable. The w3c is in charge of maintaining official web specifications Back - end technologies such as Node. Js and PHP are easily integrated.

Build a website - If you learn HTML well, you can build a website or customize an established design. Become a web developer - HTML and CSS programming is a must-have experience if you choose to pursue a career as a talented web designer.

Understand the Internet - If you'd like to improve the pace and functionality of your website, you should be familiar with HTML. Learn another language - After you've mastered the fundamentals of HTML, you'll find many other similar technologies such as JavaScript, PHP, and Angular become even simpler to grasp.

Disadvantages:

Static websites are the majority of the time. You can use PHP and JAVA for dynamic features. It prevents the consumer from implementing logic. Consequently, even though they use the same components, such as headers and footers, each web page must be generated separately. Any browsers are reluctant to implement new features.

Browser behavior may be unpredictable (for example, older browsers don't often make newer tags).

1.3 HTML's Applications

HTML is among the most commonly known programming languages on the Internet. You will study a couple of them below:

- Web page creation - HTML is a markup language that is used to generate websites. About any web page contains HTML tags, which render the page's information in a window.

- Internet Routing - HTML offers tags for navigating from one link to the next, and it is widely used for internet routing.

- Flexible UI - HTML sites already run on all platforms, including phones, tablets, desktops, and notebooks, thanks to responsive design.

- Offline access HTML pages will be made accessible remotely, mostly on the machine, without the requirement for an internet connection after they have been loaded.

- Game creation- HTML5 has built-in support for rich experiences and is now useful in game development.

1.4 HTML's Various Versions

HTML 1.0

HTML 1.0 was the first edition of HTML. It had many limitations in terms of functionality, which restricted what you're doing with your websites.

HTML 2.0

Then came HTML 2.0, which contained many HTML 1.0 and a few different ones for web design. HTML 2.0 has been the industry norm for web page design until January 1997.

HTML 3.0

HTML 2.0 performed its mission admirably, but many web page designers (also known as HTML writers or webmasters) desired greater influence of their pages and more opportunities to label up the text and improve the appearance with the sites. Netscape, the most popular browser, launched the Netscape Extension Tags, collecting new tags and attributes. Other browsers attempted to copy them, but since Netscape could not thoroughly define their new tags, they did not fit with any other browsers. When HTML developers were using these attributes and tags and then discovered that they didn't fit as intended in other browsers, it caused many frustration and issues. Around the same period, an HTML task force headed by Dave Raggett released the HTML 3.0 draught, which featured a slew of fresh and helpful features. However, only a few items from this draught were introduced in most browsers. The term "HTML 3.0 improved" soon gained popularity on the Internet but is mostly applied to documents with browser-specific tags rather than documents that followed the HTML 3.0 draft. One of the factors the draught was shelved was because of this. HTML 3.0 isn't any longer in use. Another factor HTML 3.0 didn't cut was that it was too "tall." Future versions were to be implemented in a much more "modular" manner, allowing browsers to adopt them bit by bit or modular by modular.

HTML 3.2

HTML 3.2 is the latest version of HTML (WILBUR). With the introduction of more browser-specific tags, it became clear that a new standard was needed. The W3C, which was formed in 1994 to create universal specifications for Web development, introduced the WILBUR specification, which came to be known as HTML 3.2, as a result. HTML 3.2 reflects the prescribed norm as of early 1996, and it was adopted as an accepted system in January 1997. HTML 3.2 is supported by the majority, if not all, of today's mainstream browsers.

HTML 4.0

HTML 4.0 was script COUGAR in its early days. This update adds additional features, the majority of which are derived from the now-defunct HTML 3.0 draught. In December 1997, this edition was designated as a guideline, and in April 1998, it was designated as a norm. Explorer has done an excellent job in integrating HTML 4.0's several functions. Regrettably, Netscape hasn't kept up. The new edition of Netscape Communicator also doesn't accept many of the HTML 4.0 tags and attributes. It ensures that a new website with HTML 4.0 basic tags will look fantastic in Explorer but will look terrible in Netscape.

XHTML (Extensible Hypertext Markup Language)

You'd imagine that after HTML 4.0, the next big version will be HTML 5.0, which will have a slew of different tags capable of doing all kinds of amazing stuff. It would be an excellent estimate, but it would be incorrect. After HTML 4, XHTML is the next edition of HTML. Extensible Hypertext Mark-up Language XHTML is an acronym for Configurable Hypertext Markup Language. XHTML isn't taking several different tags with it. XHTML aims to counter the latest browser innovations that are sweeping the globe. Web sites are also viewed in browsers on cell phones, automobiles, televisions, and various other hand-held digital computers and communicators. Alternative internet connectivity methods are constantly being implemented. These machines, in many situations, lack the processing capacity of a laptop or desktop machine and therefore are unable to handle weak or careless coding activities. XHTML addresses these developments. XHTML frequently addresses the requirement for disabled people (such as the blind) to provide internet connectivity. As a result, web pages published in XHTML can be used on various web and internet sites.

XHTML is the culmination of the World Wide Web Consortium's (W3C) tireless efforts to provide a format for delivering rich, high-quality web pages through a wide range of devices. In January of 2000, the World Wide Web Consortium (W3C) made XHTML an approved suggestion. XHTML is the latest version of HTML that is becoming an online standard.

HTML 5

The next version of HTML.HTML 5 (commonly abbreviated as HTML5) is the latest online format. It is based on HTML 4 (which was released in 1997) or XHTML. A lot happened on the site since the launch of HTML4, and more remains to be improved to fix all of the emerging technology and multimedia. HTML5 is the product of a collaboration between the W3C and the Internet WHATWG that started in 2006. Although HTML5 is still in progress, all of the current functionality and features are supported by the most recent browsers. HTML5's main goal is to do two things: develop the vocabulary and promote the most up-to-date multimedia. The WHATWG and W3C developed certain ground standards to do this. Reduced reliance on external sockets improved error management, and much more markup tags to substitute scripting were among them. HTML5 should be platform agnostic (that is, it should be interpreted by machines and the various applications that occur today) while still being understandable by humans.

1.5 HTML Editor

In retrospect, the HTML editor is being used to build a website's base. And just because any text editor may do the job doesn't mean you want to do it yourself. Added features, error-correcting, and an overall more intuitive editor will greatly simplify your life. HTML editors have the same fundamentals: they assist you in writing code by illustrating grammar, inserting frequently encountered HTML components and constructs, and delivering autocompletion.

Text may be converted to other languages utilizing an HTML editor, such as XML, JavaScript or CSS. However, as You all know, not everything is created equal. Some editors may be simpler to use than others, and some may have more features.

1.6 Types HTML Editor

To put it another way, still! For both novice and experienced developers, an HTML editor is essential. The main components of HTML editors, such as syntax highlighting, adding popular HTML components, and autocompletion, have already been listed. All of this ensures that the code remains usable and tidy with minimal effort, making it far simpler to be doing what you should do the best code.

If you fail to put the ending tag / in a code feature, e.g., the editor will warn you. As a result, you need not restrict yourself by not having an HTML editor.

1.7 Atom

Atom is an HTML editor released in 2014 and has gained a lot of popularity since then. The GitHub team created Atom, which is a free, accessible code editor. Atom's kit is released under a free software license and is operated by the GitHub group. It aims to give the editor a premium feel while remaining fully accessible. Often included is the ability to configure the app. In terms of the tagline, they tout themselves as an easy to hack text document for the twenty-first century. It ensures that developers can further boost Atom by editing, extending, changing, sharing the program's source code, and creating their packages.

Let's go over some of Atom's main features.

Characteristics

- Atom comes including 81 pre-installed packages and allows you to load up to 8,700 more. You may even create your software.

- A text editor that is free and open-source. The Atom editor is completely free and open-source, and it can be found on GitHub.

- Atom assists teletype. If you want to collaborate with other programmers in real-time, this is a crucial function.

- Multiple panes are supported. Atom will divide the interface into several windows, allowing you to analyze and write code in parallel.

- Intelligent autocompletion. Atoms versatile autocomplete makes you write code quicker and smarter.

- Atom is common with web developers because it is customizable. Atom is simple to customize, allowing you to change the appearance of the GUI and incorporate other useful features. You may also build your own sets and themes. Alternatively, you should easily install community-made packages and themes.

- Atom in Developer Mode You can play around with the main framework by introducing new functionality.

- Integration of Git and GitHub.

- Editing on many platforms. Atom is compatible with all operating systems.

- Atom has a sleek, premium-looking interface, as well as a live demo. Windows, Linux and Mac OS are all supported (64-bit).

1.8 Notepad ++

Notepad++ is indeed a free HTML editor designed for Windows-based computers. Wine allows Linux users to access it as well. This editor is licensed as free software, and its source code can be found on GitHub. Third-party extensions are funded, much as with other group initiatives. The versatility of Notepad++'s programming framework sets it apart. Notepad++ is very lightweight, with a smartphone edition available if you choose. Here are a few of the highlights:

Characteristics

- Notepad++ has a user interface that is plain, lightweight, and fast.

- It has a multilingual coding environment that includes ActionScript, CSS, and Visual Simple.

- Complete compliance for Windows; however, most operating systems are not allowed (without additional software.)

Why do developers like Notepad++ so much?

- It's open-source and free; • It's extensible. You may use community-created plugins or make your own.

- It's adaptable. Developers can customize the functionality and design to their liking.

- The Notepad++ GUI is easy, but developers can customize it. Windows and Linux are supported (via Wine)

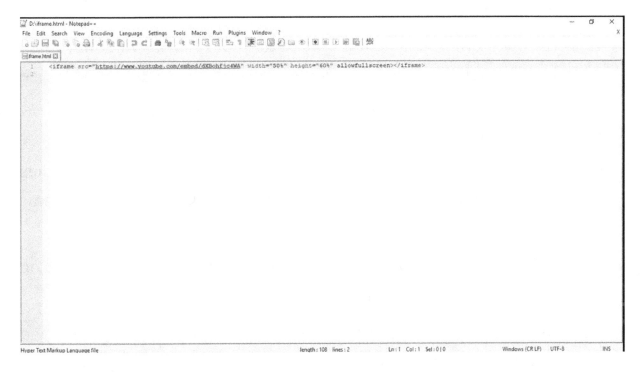

1.9 Sublime Text

Another great free HTML editor is Sublime Text. This app, which was created by either a Sydney-based company, falls into the freemium range.

Sublime text is freemium, which ensures you can download it for free but must purchase a license to use any of its functionality.

Sublime provides excellent assistance to guarantee that the package is still up to date. Users may use community-made plugins or create their own. You believe that the free edition of Sublime is sufficient. However, if you find that you want additional functionality, you can purchase the license later.

Characteristics

- Python API is supported by Sublime, allowing the plugin to extend its default features.

- Editing in real-time. You may make modifications to a large number of locations at once.

- It is cross-platform. Sublime is a text editor that runs on Windows, Linux or Mac OS X. Sublime Text 2 developers only require one license to use it on any of their machines. Sublime text is common with web developers for several reasons.

- A robust API ecosystem and package ecosystem. Thousands of bundles are accessible and designed by the group for Sublime. These programs are free and open-source.

- Editing in two sections. Developers may use several displays to work on various forms of programming at the same time.

- Go everywhere. This function is useful for quickly opening files and searching for icons, lines, or terms.

- Sublime automatically indexes the definition of Go to Any class, process, and feature in your project.

- In terms of aesthetics, the Sublime Text GUI is fantastic. Windows, Linux or Mac (32/64 bit) are both supported.

```
Test.cs                                                    UNREGISTERED

    Test.cs
1   using System;
2   using System.Collections.Generic;
3   using System.Linq;
4   using System.Text;
5   using System.Threading.Tasks;
6
7   namespace ConsoleApp1
8   {
9       class Program
10      {
11      static void Main(string[] args)
12      {
13          Console.WriteLine("Hello, this is a test!");
14          Console.ReadLine();
15      }
16      }
17  }
18

Line 18, Column 1                              Tab Size: 4        C#
```

1.10 Adobe Dreamweaver CC

Dreamweaver would be a premium, strong, and scalable tool developed and operated by software giant Adobe Inc. It offers both back-end and front-end production services. Dreamweaver is a closed-source application that is built to run inside the Adobe ecosystem. Adobe also offers tools, features, and plugins to ensure that you can write consistently. One of the editors who supports both WYSIWYG and textual approaches is Dreamweaver. So, you have the option of coding for a live video demonstration or going the traditional route.

Characteristics

- You can write code in every big programming language with Dreamweaver.

- WYSIWYG and Textual editor modes are supported.

- The Adobe app environment is fully integrated.

- Adobe Inc. provided excellent performance and assistance.

Why do web designers and developers like Adobe Dreamweaver CC?

- Create a code and test it. Developers will code when displaying the final product in this manner.

- Double-check the coding and the page's usability. This functionality will help developers adhere to the Web-Content Accessibility Guidelines more easily (WCAG.)

- Access to cloud-based creative libraries. Premium subscription to the Adobe ecosystem's vast library of assets. Colors, sentences, animations, layers, characters, and more are all included.

- Dreamweaver has a premium, high-end style about it, with a breathtaking aesthetic and architecture. After all, it's from Adobe, a well-known name inside the creative industry.

- Windows and Mac OS X are supported.

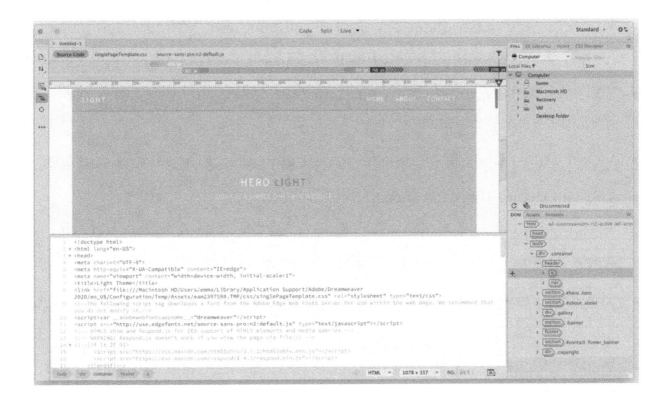

1.11 Visual Studio Code

With a vast number of customizable features, it is a free multi-code HTML editor ready to use. It takes pride in its intelligent autocomplete and other syntax answers. Visual Studio is a multi-platform and multi-language application. Its creation framework is compatible with HTML, Python, and a variety of other programming languages. It's also compliant with Microsoft Azure, allowing for simple deployment and a wide range of extensions.

Characteristics

- IntelliSense encourages you to move beyond autocomplete and syntax highlighting. It generates intelligent completions for you based on your forms, tasks, and modules.

- Features and customization. Install plugins and connect languages, styles, debuggers, and other features to your device.

- You can quickly move between different tasks thanks to the project manager's easy accessibility.

- Visual Studio Code is a favorite of web developers for several reasons.

- You can debug the code directly in the editor.

- Git commands are pre-installed. Work with Git suppliers from the editor when editing diffs, staging archives, and other files.

- The Live Server extension allows you to see a live version of your web app when editing it.

- Visual Studio has a traditional style with a clean and straightforward layout. It allows finding documents, installing a new language, and opening a new file easy. Windows x64, Linux x64 and OSX x64 are also supported.

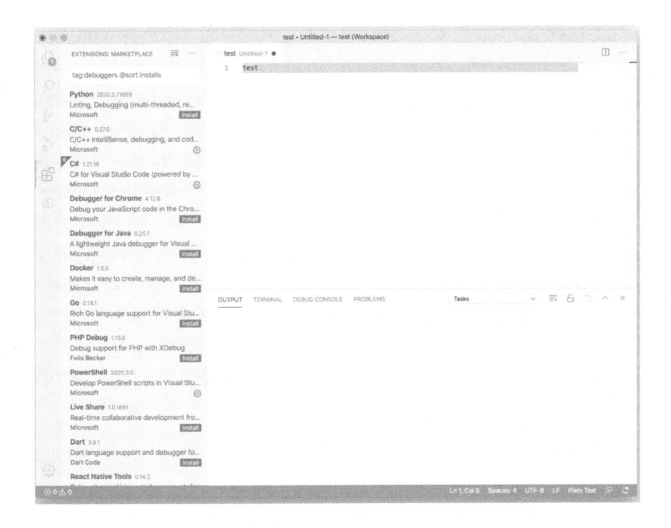

1.12 HTML statistics and figures

- Since the mid-1990s, the HTML, head, and body components were components of the HTML specification, and they were the key elements used to format HTML documents until a few years ago. Thanks to HTML5's addition of a slew of modern tags that can attach rich textual context to an HTML document's layout, the situation has improved significantly in recent years.

- HTML documents must begin with such a Document-Type Declaration (also known as a "doctype"). The doctype is used in browsers to describe the rendering mode. Since HTML5 does not describe a DTD, the doctype declaration in HTML5 is clearer and shorter.

- Since mobile browsers have completely implemented HTML5, building mobile-ready designs are as simple as designing and building for their small touch screen screens, which is why Responsive Design is so common. Some excellent meta tags enable you to customize for mobile devices as well.

- Seventy-eight percent of content creators believe the framework is appropriate for developing smartphone applications, and 68 percent believe it is appropriate for building any of all types of apps.

- HTML5 also has a slew of useful APIs for creating a smoother user interface and a more robust, dynamic web framework — here's a fast rundown of native APIs:

- Offline storage folder • Browser history tracking • Document editing • Timed video replay

- A single entity doesn't regulate HTML5. The reality is an accessible norm is one of its strongest qualities. Developers are free to let their imaginations run wild and incorporate as many features and functions as they want.

- Unlike some apps, Google Chrome ensures that any upgrade includes HTML5 support. Furthermore, YouTube's default player is already HTML5, and Google's Flash advertisements are upgraded to HTML5.

Developers' use of HTML5 (by region):

- North America uses 70 percent

- South America uses 61 percent

- ASPAC uses 60 percent

- Australia uses 60 percent

- Europe uses 59 percent

- Africa uses 50 percent

Chapter-2 Elements & Attributes in HTML

Consequent rise or properties of an entity, such as the widths and height of an image, are defined by attributes. Attributes are often defined in the opening tag and are usually name/value pairs such as name="value." Quote markers can still be used around attribute values.

Some attributes are often expected for some components. An <img> tag, for example, must have alt and src attributes. Let's glance at several explanations of how attributes should be used:

```
<image src="Scope.png" width="80" height="80" alt="School">
```

```
<a href="https://www.instagram.com/" title="HTML">
```

```
Instagram </a>
```

```
<abbr title="United States of America">USA </abbr>
```

```
input type="Integer" value="54126">
```

In the illustration above, src is an attribute within the <img> tag, and the picture path is its value. Similarly, the attribute href or within <a> tag is also an attribute, and the meaning is the relation given, and so on.

Attribute attributes may be quoted with single or double-quotes. Double quotations, on the other hand, are the most frequent. When the attribute value includes double quotes, the value must be wrapped in single quotes, for example, value='John "Williams" Jr.' In the illustration above, src is an attribute within the <img> tag, and picture path is its value. Similarly, the attribute href within the <a> tag is an attribute, and the meaning is the relation given, and so on. Attribute attributes may be quoted with single or double-quotes. Double quotations, on the other hand, are the most frequent.

When the attribute value includes double quotes, the value must be wrapped in single quotes, for example, value='John "Williams" Jr.'

A few HTML attributes don't have name/value pairs and have the name. Boolean attributes are the name for certain types of attributes. Verified, disabled, read-only, necessary, and other similar Boolean attributes are examples.

As an example

```
<input type="E-mail" required>
```

```
<Input Type= " Add" value "add" disable>
```

```
<input type="Charter" value="Read Character" read_only>
```

Many of these elements would be covered in depth in the following pages. Except for the Class and id attributes, which are case-sensitive, attribute values are usually case-insensitive. In their definition, the W3C (World Wide Web Consortium) proposes using lowercase for attribute values.

2.1 Attributes for a General Purpose

You may use certain attributes on the maximum of HTML objects, such as class, id, title and type. The following segment explains how to use them.

2.2 The "id" Attribute

An id attribute is being used to assign an entity in a document a special meaning or identifier. This allows CSS or JavaScript selection of the element much simpler.

```
<input type="Enter Text " id="First_Name">
```

```
<div id="Roll. No">
```

```
Some details </div>
```

```
<p id="information's Text">
```

```
First Paragraph. </p>
```

Within a single text, an element's id must be special. There can't be two elements of the same id in the same text because each entity can only have one id.

2.3 The class Attribute

The class attribute, like the id attribute, is used to define elements. The class attribute, unlike the id attribute, does not need to be special within the code. As seen in the following illustration, you may add a same class for multiple items in a text.

```
<input type="Enter text" class=" city">
```

```
<div class="City">New York</div>
```

```
<p class="city ">NY is beautiful city. </p>
```

Since a class may be extended to several elements, any style guidelines written for it will be assigned to any of the elements with that class.

2.4 The "style" Attribute

The style attribute enables you to define CSS styling rules directly inside the feature, such as color, font, border, and so on. To see where it operates, consider the following example:

```
<p style="color: Green;">First Paragraph. </p>
```

```
<img src="image/facebook.png " style="width: 500px;" alt="Logo">
```

```
<div style="border: 2px black ;">Facebook </div>
```

2.5 Accept Attribute

The allow attribute determines which file types the server can accept (which can be added through upload of file).

Only input <type="file"> may be used with the accept attribute. This attribute cannot be used as a validation function. On the website, file uploads must be validated.

```
<form action="/action_page.html">
```

```
<input type="file" name="picture" accepts="Photo/*">
```

```
<input type="submitted">
```

```
</form>
```

2.6 Accept-charset Attribute

The accept-charset attribute defines the word encodings that would be used when submitting the form. The reserved variable "UNKNOWN" (which means that the encoding matches the encoding of the file outlining the <form> element) is the default value.

```
<form action="/action_page.html" accept-charset=" utf-8">
```

```
First_Name: <input type="Enter text" name="F_name"><br>
```

```
Last_Name: <input type="Enter text" name="L-name"><br>
```

```
<input type="Add" value="Add">
```

```
</form>
```

2.7 "Accesskey" Attribute

The "<accesskey" attribute identifies a shortcut key used to unlock or concentrate an element. In different browsers, the shortcuts key is accessed in multiple ways.

Browser	Windows	Linux	Mac
Internet Explorer	[Alt] + *accesskey*	N/A	
Chrome	[Alt] + *accesskey*	[Alt] + *accesskey*	[Control] [Alt] + *accesskey*
Firefox	[Alt] [Shift] + *accesskey*	[Alt] [Shift] + *accesskey*	[Control] [Alt] + *accesskey*
Safari	[Alt] + *accesskey*	N/A	[Control] [Alt] + *accesskey*
Opera	Opera 15 or newer: [Alt] + *accesskey* Opera 12.1 or older: [Shift] [Esc] + *accesskey*		

2.8 The "title" Attribute

The title attribute indicates the element's title. The title attribute's syntax is identical to that of the id attribute:

This attribute's behavior is determined by the element that contains it, but it is often shown as a tooltip while the cursor passes over the component or when it is loading.

E.g.

```
<html>
<head>  < title>The tit</title> </head>
<body>
```

```
<h3 title="HTML!">It is the title</h3>
```

```
</body>
```

```
</html>
```

As a consequence, you'll get the following: It is the title.

When you hover your mouse on " It is the title, " you'll see that the title you used during your code appears as a tooltip for the cursor.

2.9 The "dir" Attribute

The "dir" attribute helps you to tell the browser which way the text can flow. As seen in the table below, the "dir" attribute will follow one of two values:

- ltr (left- right) (the default value)
- rtl Right- left (languages such as Arabic or Hebrew which are read or write right hand side to left hand side)

Example

```
<html dir="rtl">
```

```
<head>
```

```
<title>Title here</title>
```

```
</head>
```

```
<body>
```

```
The is an example from right to left
```

```
</body>
```

```
</html>
```

As a consequence, you'll get the following. It is an example from right to left. When the "dir" attribute is included in the html> tag, it controls how text is shown in the document. When included inside another tag, it directs the text for the material of that tag only.

2.10 The lang Attribute

The lang attribute lets you choose the primary language in a text, but it's just in HTML for expandable storage with older language versions. In modern XHTML papers, this attribute has been substituted by the XML: lang attribute. The lang attribute accepts ISO 639-1.two-character language codes as values. For a full set of language codes, see Codes: ISO 639-1

Example

```
<html lang="Code">
<head>
<title>HTML Page </title>
</head>
<body> This is first page of HTML </body>
</html>
```

The XML: lang Attribute is used to specify the language of a document. The XML: lang attribute takes the role of the lang attribute in XHTML. As discussed in the previous part, the type of an XML: lang attribute is an ISO-639-1 country code.

2.11 alt Attribute

Suppose a user is unable to open a picture for any purpose. In that case, the alt attribute offers alternate content (because of slow internet connection, an error in the src Parameter, or if you are using the screen reader). For the <img> variable, the alt parameter is needed. The alt attribute for <input> elements may only be used for input type="image"> elements. Use the title parameter to make a preview for a picture!

Example

```
<img src="Earth.gif" width="60" height="60" alt="Google-Map"
use-map="#Google-map">
<map name="Earth">
  <area shape="Squre" coords="10,10,182,226" href="school.htm" alt="mars">
  <area shape="rect" coords="80,158,13" href="habib0.htm" alt="Sun">
  <area shape="rect" coords="124,158,18" href="moon.htm" alt="Moon">
</map>
```

2.12 HTML elements

One of many types of HTML nodes, an HTML element is a form of Hypertext Markup Language) file part (there are comment nodes, text nodes, and others). An HTML document comprises a tree of basic HTML nodes, like HTML elements and text nodes that give the document semantics and formatting (e.g., make text bold, organize it into lists, paragraphs and embed hyperlinks or tables and images). HTML attributes may be defined for each feature. Content may also be added to elements, such as other components and text.

<HTML> (Hypertext Markup Language)

The core (top-level portion) of an Html page is described by the HTML <html> element, often known as the primary root. This aspect must be the ancestor of all other components.

<base>

The HTML <base> element specify the base URL for all relative Web addresses in a document.

<head>

Machine-readable details (metadata) about the text, such as its scripts, title and style sheets, is contained in the HTML <head> element.

<link>

The HTML External Reference Link (<link>) feature establishes a connection between the document window and an external resource. This feature is most widely used to connect to CSS, but it can also create site icons (all "favicon" type icons and symbols for the main screen and applications on mobile devices).

<meta>

Metadata which can be expressed by other HTML context items, such as foundation, relation, script, type, or title, is represented by the HTML <meta> feature.

<styling>

The HTML <style> variable specifies the style of a document or a section of a document.

\<title\>

The HTML Title variable (\<title\>) specifies the document title that appears in the title bar of a browser or the tab of a website.

2.13 Content sectioning

You may use information sectioning elements to divide the document's content into logical parts. Build a broad overview of your page's content using the sectioning elements, which provide footer and header navigation and heading elements to define content parts.

\<address\>

The HTML \<address\> aspect denotes that the embedded HTML contains contact details for individuals or groups of individuals or a business.

\<article\>

The HTML \<article\> feature denotes a self-contained structure in a book, page, program, or website intended to be distributed or reused separately (e.g., in syndication).

\<aside\>

The HTML \<aside\> aspect denotes a section of a document that material is only tangentially linked to the document's main content.

\<footer\>

The HTML \<footer\> function is used to build a footer for the sectioning root or sectioning material closest to it. A \<footer\> usually includes details regarding the section's creator, copyright information, or links to relevant documents.

<header>

The HTML <header> aspect denotes introductory text, which is usually a set of introducing or navigational aids. It may have several heading features and a badge, author name, and search form, among other stuff.

<h1>, <h2>, <h3>, <h4>, <h5>, <h6. Six stages of segment headings are described by the HTML <h1> to < h6> components. The largest segment rating is <h1>, and the lowest is <h6>.

<main>

The HTML <main> feature represents the predominant content of a document's body. The core information field contains content closely linked to or draws upon a document's or application's key focus or features.

<nav>

The HTML <nav> feature denotes a part of a website that contains navigation links, either inside the document window or to other pages. Tables of contents, Menus, and indexes are all instances of navigation pages.

<section>

The HTML <section> element describes a general isolated section of a text that isn't represented by a more complex semantic element.

2.14 Text content

In between <body> opening and </body> closing tags, use HTML text modules to arrange blocks or pieces of content. These elements define the intent or layout of the material, which is essential for usability and SEO.

<blockquote>

The HTML <blockquote> Item (Block Quote Element) denotes an expanded quotation. Indentation is a popular visual representation of this (Notes for how to edit it). The cite attribute can provide a URL for the quotation's source, while the cite function can allow the source's writing.

<dd>

In a description list, the HTML <dd> variable offers a description, meaning, or significance for the preceding word (dt) (dl).

<div>

The standard container for flow material is the HTML Data Division feature (<div>). Unless it's styled with CSS, it has little influence on the material or structure (e.g., styling can be applied to it).

<dl>

A summary list is represented by the HTML <dl> variable. The element contains a set of term classes (specified with the <dt> element) as well as definitions (provided by <dt> elements). This feature is often used to introduce a dictionary or view metadata (a list of pair key-value).

<dt>

The HTML <dt> object is used to specify a concept in a summary or specification list and that it must be used within an <dl> element.

<figcaption>

A tag or legend detailing the remainder of its parent figure item attributes is represented either by HTML <figcaption> or the "Figure Caption" element.

<figure>

The <figure> tag in HTML is used to represent a statistic. The (Figure with Alternate Caption) element denotes self-contained material that may have an optional caption defined by the <figcaption> element.

<hr>

A thematic split between paragraph-level items is represented by the HTML <hr> element: a changing scene in a tale or a shift of subject within a segment.

< li>

The li> element in HTML is used to display a list object.

<ol>

An organized list of items is represented by the HTML <ol> variable, usually represented as a numbered list.

<p>

A paragraph is represented by the HTML <p> variable.

<pre>

The HTML <pre> node denotes preformatted text that should be shown as it appears in the HTML code.

<ul>

The unordered list of objects, usually made as a bulleted list, is represented by the HTML <ul> variable.

2.15 Inline text semantics

The HTML inline content semantic was used to describe the context, form, or style of an expression, line, or another random piece of text.

<a>

The href attribute on the HTML <a> tag (or anchor element) provides a hyperlink to internet sites, directories, email addresses, page locations, or something else a URL may answer.

<abbr>

An acronym or abbreviation is represented by the HTML Abbreviation feature (<abbr>). The additional title attribute may include an expansion or definition for the abbreviation.

<b>

The HTML Bring More attention to component (<b>) is used to attract the viewer's interest to material that isn't given special emphasis elsewhere.

<bdi>

The HTML two-directional Isolate feature (<bdi>) instructs the bidirectional algorithm in the browser to handle the text it includes separately from the surrounding text.

<bdo>

The HTML two-directional script Override feature (bdo>) overrides the text's current directionality and renders the text in a separate direction.

The <br> feature in HTML creates a line break in document (carriage-return). It's helpful when writing poetry or an address where the line division is essential.

<cite>

The HTML Citation feature (<cite>) is used to denote a connection to a cited artistic work, and the title of the work must be included.

<code>

The HTML <code> feature styles its contents to show that the document is a short piece of computer code.

<data>

The <data> feature in HTML connects a piece of text to a machine-readable translation. The time factor must be used whether the material is time or date-related.

<dfn>

The HTML Description variable (<dfn>) denotes the word being described as a defining word or sentence.

<em>

The HTML <em> aspect denotes text with a strong focus on it. The <em> aspect may be nesting, with each level representing a higher level of focus.

<i>

The HTML Idiomatic Content feature You will learn various texts separated from the regular text for various reasons, such as conversational data, technical terminology, and taxonomic designations.

<kbd>

The HTML Keyboard Input feature (<kbd>) denotes voice input, text input from the user from a keyboard, or some other data entry system with a period of inline text.

<Mark>

According to the identified passage's significance or significance in the enclosing sense, the HTML Label Text element (<mark>) reflects text labeled or highlighted for comparison or notation purposes.

<q>

The embedded text is a small inline quote, as indicated by the HTML <q> feature. The majority of current browsers do this by enclosing the document in quotation marks.

<rb>

The HTML Ruby Base (<rb>) feature separates the base text portion of a ruby annotation, which is annotated.

<rp>

The HTML Ruby Back - up Parenthesis (<rp>) element is being used to include back - up parentheses for browsers that don't accept the ruby element for displaying ruby annotations.

<rt>

The ruby text part of a ruby notation is specified by the HTML Ruby Text (<rt>) variable used to offer transcription, translation, or pronunciation details for East Asian fonts. The <rt> variable must be stored inside a ruby element at all times.

\<rtc\>

The HTML Ruby Script Folder (\<rtc\>) module includes symbolic annotations for characters in ruby of \<rb\> items included inside a ruby element. Both semantic (\<rtc\>) and pronunciation (\<rt\>) are possible for \<rb\> objects.

\<ruby\>

Tiny annotations made below, above, or next to base text are represented by the HTML \<ruby\> feature, which is typically used to display the pronunciation of Asian characters. It may also be used to annotate other document types, but this is a less popular use.

\<s\>

Text with such a strikethrough, and a line across it, is rendered using the HTML \<s\> feature. To reflect items that are no longer meaningful or correct, use the \<s\> variable. When signaling document edits, however, \<s\> is not appropriate; instead, use the ins and del components, as required.

\<samp\>

The HTML Sample Element (samp\>) is used to encapsulate inline text that reflects a computer program's sample (or quoted) output.

\<small\>

Independent of its modeled presentation, the HTML \<small\> analysis results from side-comments and fine print, such as copyright and legal documents. By contrast, it reduces the font size of the text inside it by one size, for example, from tiny to x-small.

\<snap\>

The HTML \<span\> feature is a common inline box for phrasing material that doesn't reflect something by itself. It may be used to individuals belonging for style (using id attributes or the class) or because they have similar attribute values, such as lang.

<strong>

The HTML Strong Value Element (<strong>) denotes a high level of significance, severity, or urgency in the text. The contents are usually shown in the bold format in browsers.

< sub>

The HTML Subscript variable (<sub>) defines the inline text that should be shown as the subscript for no other purpose than typography.

<sup>

The HTML Superscript feature (<sup>) defines the inline text that should be shown as a superscript for no other purpose than typography.

<time>

The HTML <time> aspect denotes a particular time frame.

<u>

The Html Unarticulated Notation feature (<u>) represents a block of inline text that should be made with a non-textual annotation.

<var>

In a mathematical model or a programming context, the HTML Vector element (<var>) reflects the value of a variable.

<wbr>

The HTML <wbr> feature denotes a word break chance, a spot inside text where the browser will break a line even though its line-breaking laws will not otherwise break a line there.

2.16 Elements of Styling HTML

Whenever it comes to web page presentation, HTML is very minimal. It was created to be a concise way of presenting facts. Cascading Style Sheets created by W3C in December 1996 to make it easier to style HTML objects. Size and typeface for fonts, colors for text and backgrounds, arrangement of text and pictures, amount of space between border, elements and outline for elements, and various other style properties are made much easier with CSS.

2.17 Adding Styles

Style material may be added as a text file or incorporated directly into the HTML document. The three methods for adding style details to an HTML text are as follows.

- Embedded style — Uses the <style> feature in the document's head portion.
- External CSS file — This is accomplished using the <link> feature to refer to an external Style sheet.

You will go through each of these various styles of style sheets one by one in this book

External type sheets have the least concern, while style sheets get the largest. The embedded style sheet's contrasting style guidelines may take precedence over the style attribute if you define your descriptions in integrated and external CSS sheets.

2.18 Inline Styles

By placing the CSS rules immediately into the start tag, inline styles have been used to add specific guidelines to an element. The style attribute may be used to apply it to an aspect.

A set of CSS assets and meaning pairs are used in the type attribute. A semicolon (;) separates each property: value pair, much like you might appear in an integrated or exterior style sheet. However, it must all fit on one side, with no line breaks after the semicolon.

The following example shows how to change the text's color and font size:

Example

```
<h1 style="color:Blue ; font-size:29 px;">Heading </h1>
<p style="color:Yellow ; font-size:20 px;"> paragraph.</p>
<div style="color:Red ; font-size:16px;">Text </div>
```

Using inline patterns is commonly thought to be a poor idea. Since style guidelines are inserted directly within the html tag, the presentation is mingled with the document's text, making modifying and managing a website extremely challenging.

2.19 Embedded-Style Sheets

Internal style sheets, also known as embedded style sheets, only influence the paper in which they are embedded.

The <style> tag in an HTML document's head segment is used to describe embedded style sheets. Inside the <head> segment, you can specify any number of <styles> components.

The illustration below shows how style guidelines are incorporated into a web page.

Example

```
<head>
<style>
body { background-color: Yellow; }
h1 {color: Red; }
p { color: black; }
</style>
</head>
```

2.20 External-Style Sheets

If a pattern is extended to a large number of websites, an additional style sheet is ideal.

An external style sheet is a different document that contains all of the style rules, which can be linked from any Html file on your Web. External-style sheets seem to be the most versatile since they enable you to update only one file to alter the appearance of a whole website. External style sheets may be attached in two ways, connecting and importing

2.21 External-Style Sheets Are Linked

The <link> tag may be used to link an external-style sheet to an HTML text. As seen here, the <link> tag is placed within the <head> section:

Example

```
<head>
<link rel="CSS" href="html.css">
</head>
```

2.22 Importing External-Style Sheets

Another way to load an external-style sheet is to use the import rule. The import declaration tells the browser to install and use the styles from an external style sheet.

It can be seen in two forms. The easiest method is to have it in your <head> section's <style> feature. Other CSS rules can also be included in the <style> function, so keep that in mind.

Example

```
<style>
  @import URL ("html/CS.css");
  p {  color: Red;  font-size: 18px; }
</style>
```

Similarly, the @import clause may be used to insert a style sheet onto another style sheet.

Example

```
@import URL("HTML/guideline.css");
body
{
```

```
color: Red; font-size: 18px;
}
```

Chapter-3 HTML for Text Formatting

HTML contains many tags that you can use to render certain data on your websites to look different than regular text, like the following.

3.1 Bold Text (<b>)

You will see in the below example, everything that occurs inside the <b>...</b> variable is bolded.

```
 html>
<head> <title>Text Title for bold</title> </head>
<body>
<p> The is an example for <b>bold</b> text. </p>
</body>
</html>
```

It produced the result as "This is an example for **bold** text.

3.2 Italic Text (<i>)

Anything contained inside the <i>...</i> variable is italicized, as seen below.

```
<html>
<head> <title>Title for Italic</title>  </head>
<body>
<p>It is an example for <i>italicized</i> text. </p>
</body>
```

```
</html>
```

It will produce "It is an example for the *italicized* text."

3.3 Underlined Text (<u>)

All that occurs inside the <u>...</u> aspect is underlined, as seen below.

```
<html>
```
```
<head> <title>Title of Underlined </title> </head>
```
```
<body>
```
```
<p>It is an example of <u>under-lined</u> Text. </p>
```
```
</body>
```
```
</html>
```

It will produce a result "It is an example of **under-line** text."

3.4 Strike Text (<strike>)

Strikethrough is used to view something that occurs inside the <strike>...</strike> element, which is a fine line across the text as seen below.

```
<html>
```
```
<head>
```
```
<title>Title strike Text </title>
```
```
</head>
```
```
<body> <p>It is an example of <strike>strike</strike> text. </p>
```

```
</body>
```

```
</html>
```

It will produce a result "It is an example of ~~strike~~ text."

3.5 Monospaced Font (<tt>)

A <tt>...</tt> element's content is composed in monospaced font. Since various letters have different height (for example, the letter's' is larger than the letter, fonts are classified as variable-width fonts). Each letter in a monospaced text, on the other hand, is the same distance.

```
<html>
```

```
<head>  <title> Title for Monospaced </title>  </head>
```

```
<body>
```

```
<p>It is an example of <tt>monospaced</tt> text. </p>
```

```
</body>
```

```
</html>
```

It will produce the result "It is an example of monospaced text."

3.6 Superscript Text (<sup>)

The text of a ^{...} variable is composed in superscript; the fonts is the same as the surrounding characters, except it is shown halves a character's height over them.

```
<html>
```

```
<head><title>Title for Super_script</title></head>
```

```
<body><p>It is an example of <sup>super_script</sup>text.</p>
```

```
</body>
```

```
</html>
```

It will produce a result. "It is an example of ^{superscript} text

3.7 Subscript Text (<sub>)

A _{...} element's text is typed in subscript; the text size is the same as the surrounding characters, but it is shown halves a character's height under the other characters.

```
<html>
```

```
<head> <title>Title Subscript </title> </head>
```

```
<body>
```

```
 <p>It is an example of <sub>subscript</sub> text. </p>
```

```
</body>
```

```
</html>
```

It will produce a result "It is an example of _{subscript} text."

3.8 Inserted Text (<ins>)

 Inserted text is something that occurs inside the ins>.../ins> element.

```
<html>
```

```
<head> <title> Title for Inserted Text</title> </head>
```

```
<body>
```

```
<p>It is an example of <del>delete</del> <ins>inserted </ins> text </p>
```

```
</body>
```

```
</html>
```

It will produce a result "It is an example of inserted text."

3.9 Deleted Text (<del>)

All text inside the <del>...</del> function is shown as removed text.

```
<html>
```

```
<head> <title>Deleted </title> </head>
```

```
<body>
```

```
<p>It is an example of <del>delete</del> <ins>and inserted </ins> text
</p>
```

```
</body>
```

```
</html>
```

It will produce a result "It is an example of inserted text."

3.10 Larger Text (<big>)

The text of the <big>...</big> feature is one font size greater than that of the remaining of the text containing it.

```
<html>
```

```
<head> <title>Title for larger text</title> </head>
```

```
<body>
```

```
<p>It is an example of <big>larger</big>text. </p>
```

```
</body>
```
```
</html>
```

It will produce a result "It is an example of larger text."

3.11 Smaller Text (<small>)

The text of the <small>...</small> feature is one font smaller size than that of the remaining text surrounding it.

```
<html>
```
```
<head> <title> Title for small text </title> </head>
```
```
<body>
```
```
p>It is an example of <small>small</small >text. </p></body>
```
```
</html>
```

It will produce a result "It is an example of small text."

3.12 Grouping Content (<div> <span>)

You may use the <div> and <span> elements to link elements together to construct parts or sections of a list.

E.g. all of the endnotes on a website may be included inside a <div> element to show that all of the items inside that <div> element are related to the footnotes. You may then apply a style to the <div> feature to make them look according to a collection of guidelines.

```
<html>
```
```
<head> <title>The Example</title> </head>
```

```
<body>

<div id = "List" align = "middle" >

<a href = "/index.htm">Page</a> |

<a href = "/about/contact_us.htm">Phone</a> |

<a href = "/about/index.htm">Why US</a>

</div>

<div id = "content" align = "left" >

<h5>HTML programming</h5>

<p>Just a practice.....</p>

</div>

</body>

</html>
```

It will produce the result

Page | Phone | Why US

HTML programming

Just a practice.....

In contrast, the <span> element is only used to combine inline objects. If you have a section of a paragraph that you want to combine together, you may do so with the <span> function, as seen below.

```
<html>

<head> <title>Span </title> </head>
```

```
<body>
<p>It is the example of <span style = "color: Purple">span_tag</span>
and the <span style = "color: red">div tag</span> along with .CSS</p>
</body>
</html>
```

It will produce the following result

It is the example of the span tag and the div tag along with CSS

3.12 Emphasized Text (<em>)

Everything that appears within the <em>...</em> element is highlighted text.

```
<html>
<head> <title> Title for Emphasized Text</title> </head>
<body>
<p>It is an example of  <em>emphasized</em> text.</p>
</body>
</html>
```

It shows the result "It is an example of *emphasized* text."

3.13 Marked Text (<mark>)

Anything inside the <mark>...</mark> feature is labelled with Red ink and shown as such.

```
<html>
<head> <title>Title of Marked Text</title> </head>
<body> <p>It is an example of <mark>marked</mark> with Red </p>
</body>
</html>
```

It will produce the result "It is an example of marked with a red."

3.14 Strong Text (<strong>)

All inside the <strong>...</strong> aspect is treated as essential text.

```
<html>
<head> <title> Title of Strong </title> </head>
<body>
<p>It is an example of <strong>strong</strong> text. </p>
</body>
</html>
```

It will produce a result

It is an example of **strong** text.

3.15 Abbreviation (<abbr>)

Placed a text within the opening <abbr> and closing </abbr> tags to abbreviate it. If current, the title element must only include this complete summary.

```
<html>

<head> <title>Abbreviation's title</title> </head>

<body>

<p>It is an example of abbreviation <abbr title = "United states of America">USA</abbr>. </p>

</body>

</html>
```

It will produce a result "It is an example of abbreviation USA."

3.16 Text Direction (<bdo>)

Bi-Directional Override <bdo>...</bdo> is an element that is used to bypass that current text direction.

```
<html>

<head> <title>Title of Direction</title> </head>

<body>

<p>Test Text L-R. </p>

<p><bdo dir = "rtl">Text R-L. </bdo></p>

</body>

</html>
```

It will produce the result

Test from left to right.

.tfel ot thgir txeT

3.17 Special Terms (<dfn>)

You should use the <dfn>...</dfn> component (or HTML Description Element) to indicate that you're adding a new word. It's equivalent to using italics in the middle of a document. The <dfn> function is typically used to introduce a main word for the first time. The text of a <dfn> element is usually rendered in italic font in modern browsers.

```
<html>
<head><title>Title Special</title></head>
<body>
<p>It is an example
</body>
</html>
```

It will produce "It is an example of *special* Text."

3.18 Quoting Text (<blockquote>)

If you wish to quote something from another source, place it between the <blockquote>...</blockquote> tags. Text within a blockquote> feature is normally indented from the surrounding text's left and right sides, and italicized font is often used.

```
<html>
<head>
<title>Title Blockquote</title>
</head>
```

```
<body>
```

```
<p> First, it is a good idea to maintain order and structure in your HTML documents. </ p>
```

```
<blockquote> Avoid overloading your pages with heavy images and other fancy stuff you have found on the Internet. </blockquote>
```

```
</body>
```

```
</html>
```

It will produce a result

First, it is a good idea to maintain order and structure in your HTML documents.

> Avoid overloading your pages with heavy images and other fancy stuff you have found on the Internet.

3.19 Short Quotations (<q>)

When you want to insert a double quotation within a sentence, use the <q>...</q> feature.

```
<html>
```

```
<head><title>Title</title></head>
```

```
<body>
```

```
<p>It is an example, <q>Double Quotations</q>.</p>
```

```
</body>
```

```
</html>
```

It will produce a result

It is an example, "Double Quotations."

3.20 Text Citations (<cite>)

If you're citing something, you should put the source between the opening <cite> and closing </cite> tags.

The output of the <cite> feature is made in italicized text by contrast, as it would be in a print publication.

```
<html>
<head> <title>Title</title> </head>
<body>
<p>It is an example <cite>Text citations</cite>. </p>
</body>
</html>
```

It will produce the result. "It is an example *Text citation.*"

3.21 Computer Code (<code>)

All programming code that will occur on a Website page should be enclosed by a <code>...</code> extension. The <code> element's material is usually displayed in a monospaced text.

```
<html>
<head> <title>Title of Code </title> </head>
<body>
<p>Text. <code>It is an example code. </code> Text. </p>
</body>
```

```
</html>
```

It will produce the result. "Text. It is an example code. Text."

3.22 Keyboard Text (<kbd>)

If you're talking about computers, you can use the <kbd>...</kbd> element to mean what must be typed in, as in this case.

```
<html>
```

```
<head> <title>Title Keyboard</title></head>
```

```
<body>
```

```
<p>Text. <kbd>It is an example </kbd> Text. </p>
```

```
</body>
```

```
</html>
```

It will produce a result Text. It is an example Text."

3.23 Programming Variables (<pre> <code>)

This element is usually used in conjunction with the <pre> and <code> components to indicate that the form of the function is a vector.

```
<html>
```

```
<head> <title>Title For Example</title> </head>
```

```
<body>
```

```
<p><code>File. Code ("<var>User. Name </var>")</code></p>
```

```
</body>
```

```
</html>
```

It will produce the result "File. Code ("*User. Name* ")"

3.24 Program Output (<samp>)

The <samp>...</samp> variable specifies a sample result from a software, document, or other source. It's mostly used to log programming and coding principles.

```
<html>
<head> <title>Title Example</title> </head>
<body>
<p>It is an example a program <samp>Output </samp></p>
</body>
</html>
```

It will produce the result "It is an example of a program output Output!"

3.25 Address Text (<address>)

Any address is contained in the <address>...</address> element.

```
<html>
<head> <title>Address Title </title> </head>
<body>
<address>B-IV 451 street 4 New York USA </address>
</body>
```

```
</html>
```

It will produce "*B-IV 451 street 4 New York USA*"

3.26 Acronym (<acronym>)

You will use the <acronym> element tag to show that the text within the <acronym> and </acronym> Tags is an acronym. Typically, several browsers do not alter the appearance of the <acronym> element's material.

```
<html>
<head> <title>Title of Acronym </title> </head>
<body>
<p>It is an example of <acronym> acronym </acronym></p>
</body>
</html>
```

It will show the result "It is an example of the acronym."

3.27 Comments

A comment would be a block of code that no web viewer displays. It is common sense to include comments in the HTML document file, particularly when working with complicated HTML documents. Comments are used to denote the different parts of an Html file and some other details regarding the code that might be useful to someone working at the code. Comments also aid in the understanding of the code by yourself and others and increase the readability of your code.

Between the !—... --> tags, HTML comments are held. As a result, any code or note inserted inside the !—... --> tags will be immediately interpreted as a comment, and the browser will disregard it and not show it.

```
<html>
<head> <! --Started header here-->
<title> Title here </title>
</head> <! – Header End -->
<body>
<p>Html coding here.... </p>
</body>
</html>
```

It will show the result "Html coding here..."

If you have noticed in the code, you placed the certain text in between the comment tag and when you check the output, it doesn't get displayed in the document. The browser did not display it because it read it as a comment so it ignored it when it was displaying the rest of the content.

3.28 HTML Comment Types and Formats

HTML comments come in a variety of forms and formats, including:

- Conditional Comments
- Comment Suffix
- Multiline Comments
- Commenting Style
- Commenting Script

Chapter-4: HTML Images, Tables, list and blocks

Images, list blocks, and tables are essential for creating Html files and straightforwardly describing several abstract topics on your website. In this part, you'll go into how to use photos on web pages in easy steps.

4.1 Insert Image

Using the <img> suffix, you may add any picture to your web page. The basic syntax for using this HTML tag is as follows.

```
<img src = "URL of image" ... attributes/>
```

The <img> is a void tag, that ensures it can only include a certain set of attributes and has no closing tag.

```
<html>
<head><title> Image in Page</title>
</head>
<body><p>Image-Insert</p>
<img src = "Google/axy.png" alt = "Image" />
</body>
</html>
```

You may use a JPEG, GIF or PNG image file depending on your preference; make sure the src attribute contains the right image file name. The picture name is case sensitive at all times. The <alt> HTML attribute is a required element attribute that specifies an alternative text for the picture if it cannot be viewed due to a network issue.

4.2 Set Image Location

You usually hold all of the photographs in a separate directory. So, let's put your Html document image.html in your home directory and make a subdirectory image within the home directory for our test.png document.

```html
<html>
<head> <title>Image in page</title>
</head>
<body> <p>Simple Image Insert</p>
<img src = "thegoogleicon.png" alt = "Image" />
</body>
</html>
```

4.3 Set the image's width and height.

The height and width attributes enable you to dynamically define the height and width of a picture depending on how you would like it to look. You may also specify the image's width and height in pixels or as a percentage of the actual dimension.

```html
<html>
<head>
<title> width and height. </title></head>
<body> <p> width and height. </p>
<img src = "thegoogleicon.png" alt = "Image" width = "250" height = "120"/>
</body>
```

4.4 Image Border

The picture would have some kind of borders around it by default; however, you may directly set the border depth of the image using the borders attribute of the <img> class. Giving an image a thickness of zero, for example, implies there would be no boundary around the image.

```html
<html>
 <head>
    <title>Image Border</title></head>
<body><p> image Border</p>
<img src = "thegoogleicon.png" alt = "Image" border = "5"/>
</body>
</html>
```

4.5 HTML Tables

Tables in HTML enable web developers to view data in columns and rows of table cells, such as text, photos, connections, and other tables. The <table> HMTL tag is used to construct HTML tables, with the <tr> tag used to create table rows and the <td> tag used to create table data cells. All of the elements under <td> are standard and, by contrast, left-aligned.

```html
<html> <head>
<title>Title_Tables</title></head>
```

```
<body><table_border = "2">
```

```
<tr><td>R-A, C-A</td><td>R-B, C-B</td>
```

```
</tr><tr><td>R-B C-A</td><td>R-B, C-B</td></tr>
```

```
</table>
```

```
</body>
```

```
</html>
```

It will show the result

R-1, C-1	R-2, C-2
R-2, C-1	R-2, C-2

The border text within the table tag is an element of the <table> tag in this case, and it's used to apply a border to all of the table cells as defined in the border attribute. If a border isn't what you're looking for, just use border = "0."

4.6 Table Heading

The <th> tag may be used to describe the table heading. As a result, this tag would be used to substitute the <td> tag, which is primarily used to reflect the table data cell. You can always make your tabletop row the table heading, as seen in the illustration below. Otherwise, you may use the <th> variable in either row. The default behavior of headings specified in the <th> tag is for them to be oriented and bold.

```
<html>
```

```
<head>
```

```
<title>Table Heading </title> </head>

<body>

<table border = "2">

<tr><th>St-Name</th><th>marks</th></tr>

<tr><td>Ali Raman</td><td>500</td></tr>

<tr><td>Ali Hussain</td><td>890</td></tr></table>

</body>

</html>
```

It will show the result

St-Name	marks
Ali Raman	500
Ali Hussain	890

4.7 Cellpadding and Cells pacing Attributes

To set the blank space in the table cells, you'll use two attributes named cell-spacing and cell-padding. The cell spacing property specifies the distance between cell-padding and table cells, specifies the distance between a cell's boundaries and its text.

```
<html>

<head><title>Cellpadding</title>

</head>

<body>

<table border = "2" cellpadding = "12" cellspacing = "12">
```

```
<tr><th>St.Name</th><th>Marks</th></tr>

<tr> <td>Ali Raman</td><td>580</td></tr>

<tr><td>Ali Hussain</td><td>980</td></tr>

</table> </body> </html>
```

It will show the following result.

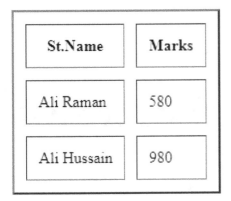

4.8 HTML List

Web developers have three options for viewing data-filled lists in HTML. One or even more list elements are required in all HTML lists. Lists may include the following items:

• <ul> (unordered list): Using simple bullets to represent objects in lists.

• <ol>: A numbered list. To show your list info, this uses a variety of numbers.

• <dl>: A compilation of definitions. It organizes the list of objects in the same way a dictionary does.

4.9 HTML Unordered Lists

The unordered lists are a set of similar objects that are not arranged or sequenced in any particular way. The HTML <ul> tag may be used to construct this kind of list. A bullet is shown next to each object in the unordered chart.

```
<html>
 <head>
<title>Unordered</title>
</head><body>
<ul><li>          Chapter-1</li>          <li>Chapter-2</li><li>Chapter-3</li>
<li>Chapter-4</li>  </ul>
</body>
</html>
```

It will show the result as

- Chapter-1
- Chapter-2
- Chapter-3
- Chapter-4

4.10 The type listing attribute

It is a HTML attribute for the <ul> tag that specifies the bullet type you want the list items to have. A disc is the default list form. The following are also the bullet styles that are available:

```
<ul type = "Circle"><ul type = "disc"> <ul type = "Square">
<html>
<head><title>Title of Unordered</title></head>
```

```html
<body>
<ul type = "square">
<li>Chapter-1</li> <li>Chapter-2</li>
<li>Chapter-3</li> <li>Chapter-4</li>
</ul>
<ul type = "disc">
<li>Chapter-5</li><li>Chapter-6</li>
<li>Chapter-7</li><li>Chapter-8</li>
</ul>
<ul type = "circle">
<li>Chapter-9</li><li>Chapter-10</li>
<li>Chapter-11</li><li>Chapter-12</li>
</ul>
</body></html>
```

- Chapter-1
- Chapter-2
- Chapter-3
- Chapter-4

- Chapter-5
- Chapter-6
- Chapter-7
- Chapter-8

o Chapter-9
o Chapter-10
o Chapter-11
o Chapter-12

4.11 HTML Ordered Lists

If you like to see the lists in an amount or sorted layout instead of unordered or bulleted, use the HTML organized list file. This set was made with the <ol> HTML tag. The numbering of the list begins at one and continues to grow for each subsequent organized list component with the <li> tag.

```
<html> <head>
<title> Ordered List</title>
</head>
<body><ol>
<li>Chapter-1</li><li>Chapter-2</li>
<li>Chapter-3</li><li>Chapter-1</li>
</ol></body>
</html>
```

1. Chapter-1
2. Chapter-2
3. Chapter-3
4. Chapter-1

Chapter-5: Links, Fonts, Multimedia, Frames & Iframes

In this chapter, you will learn Links, Fonts, Multimedia, Frames & Iframes in HTML.

5.1 Text Links

A website also includes several links that lead to other sites or even separate parts of the same page. Hyperlinks are the different types of links.

Hyperlinks enable users to navigate different websites on the Internet by simply clicking on terms, sentences, or images. As a result, you'll learn how to build hyperlinks from text or photographs on a webpage.

5.2 Linking Documents

An HTML tag is used to specify a connection. This tag is known as the anchor tag, and everything between the starting tag and the terminating tag becomes a component of the connection, which a user may press to access the connected text. The basic notation for using tag is as follows.

```
<html>
<head> <title> Linking Documents </title> </head>
<body> <p>Just Click</p>
<a href = "https://www.facebook.com" target = "FB">Facebook</a>
</body>
</html>
```

5.3 Target Attributes

In our previous case, you made use of the goal attribute. This attribute defines the condition in which the associated document is opened. The below are the possibilities:

- blank: The associated Text would be opened in a new tab
- self: It opens the related text in the same window as the current one.
- Parent: It will open the file in the parent window that is connected.
- top: This will show the associated text in the window's whole body.
- Open the linked file in a specified target window with this option.

```html
<html>
<head>
<title>Title for example </title>
<base href = "https://www.google.com/"></head>
<body>      <p>Just Click </p>
<a href = "/html/Facebook.htm" target = "_blank">Opens in New</a>
</body>
</html>
```

5.4 Base Path

It is unnecessary to include a whole URL for each connection when linking HTML documents to an analogous website. If you use the <base> tag in the File header, you'll be able to avoid it. This tag is used to include a common route for all connections. As a result, your browser can combine the assigned relative path with the current base path to form an entire URL.

```html
<html>
```

```
<head>
```

```
<title>Title for example </title>
```

```
<base href = "https://www.google.com/"></head>
```

```
<body><p>Just Click </p>
```

```
<a href = "/html/Facebook.htm" target = "_blank">Opens in New</a>
```

```
</body>
```

```
</html>
```

Linking to a Section of a Page. The name attribute may be used to build a path to a certain portion of a webpage. It's a two-step procedure.

To begin, build a connection to the location you want to visit inside a website and label it by using the tag as follows:

```
<h1>Linking <a name = "Bottom"></a></h1>
```

The second move is to create a hyperlink between the text and the location where you want to go:

```
<a href = "www.google.com">Go to the Bottom</a>
```

5.5 Link Colors setting

Using the connect, vlink and alink, attributes of the <body> tag, you can actually determine the colors of your active and visited links.

```
<html>
```

```
<head> <title>Linking Title </title>
```

```
<base href = "https://google.com/">
```

```
</head>
```

```
<body alink = "#256850" link = "#141414" vlink = "#F41533">
<p>Click</p>
<a href = "www.google.com" target = "_blank" >HTML link</a>
</body>
</html>
```

5.6 HTML Fonts

Fonts are critical to rendering a web more user-friendly and improving page readability. The font face and color are largely dependent on the device and browser being used to display your article; however, you can style, scale, and color the text on your site using the HTML <font> suffix. A <basefont> tag may make all text the same height, face, and color.

To configure the fonts, use the Font Tag's height, color, and face attributes. Simply use the font> tag to modify all of the typeface attributes on your website at any time. The text after that would not alter until you close the tag with the </font> tag. Inside a single <font> tag, you can modify one or more of the font attributes.

5.7 Set Font Size

The size attribute may be used to change the font size of the text. The agreed values vary from 1 (smallest) to 7 (largest) (largest). A font's default size is three.

```
<html>
<head> <title>Font_Size</title></head>
```

```html
<body><font size="7">size ="7"</font><br />
<font size = "6">size = "6"</font><br />
<font size = "5">Size = "5"</font><br />
<font size = "4">size= "4"</font><br />
<font size = "3">size ="3"</font><br />
<font size = "2">size = "2"</font><br />
<font size = "1">size = "1"</font>
</body>
</html>
```

size = "7"

size = "6"

Size = "5"

size = "4"

size = "3"

size = "2"

size = "1"

5.8 Relative Font Size

You may choose how many sizes bigger or smaller the font should be than the norm. You may use font size = <"-n"> or font size =< "+n"> to define the font size.

```
<html>
```

```
<head><title>Font_Style</title></head>
```

```
<body><font size="+4">size ="+4"</font><br />
<font size="+3">size="+3"</font><br />
<font size="+2">size="+2"</font><br />
<font size = "+1">size = "+1"</font><br />
<font size ="-1">size ="-1"</font>
</body></html>
```

size = "+4"

size = "+3"

size = "+2"

size = "+1"

size = "-1"

5.9 Font Face Setting

You may use the face attribute to change the glyph face, but keep in mind that if the consumer will not have the font enabled, they didn't manage to see it. Instead, the consumer would be presented with the computer's default font face.

```
<html>
```

```
<head><title>Face_font </title></head>
```

```
<body>
```

```
<font face ="Times New Roman" size = "5">Times New Roman</font><br />
```

```
<font face="Bed_rock"size="5">Bed_rock</font><br />
```

```
</body></html>
```

Times New Roman
Bedrock

5.10 Font Color Setting

The colour attribute within the font> tag may be used to change the colour of your font while it is shown. You may also define the colour you like by typing in the name of a colour or its hex code.

```
<html>
```

```
<head>
```

```
<title>Font Color</title></head><body>
```

```
<font color = "#FF0000">This text is in pink</font><br />
```

```
<font color = "Blue">This text is Blue</font>
</body>
</html>
```

This text is in pink
This text is Blue

5.11 HTML – Frames

HTML frames are often used to divide the browser window into several parts, each of which can view and load a different HTML document. A frameset is a collection of frames inside a browser window. The window is divided into frames in the same manner as the tables are divided into rows and columns.

5.12 Disadvantages of Frames

There are a few drawbacks of using frames in your web pages so that you can avoid them at all costs:

- Certain smaller computers are unable to handle frames because their screens are insufficiently wide to separate.
- Because of differences in screen resolutions, your page can appear differently on different computers.
- The back button on the browser would not function as anticipated.
- Frame technology is still not supported by a lot of browsers.

5.13 Creating Frames

You use the <frameset> tag instead of the <body> tag use the frames. The <frameset> tag specifies how the window can be divided into frames. Horizontal frames are defined by the row's attributes of the <frameset> suffix, whereas the cols attribute defines vertical frames. Each frame is identified by the <frame> tag, which specifies which HTML document will be shown in the frame.

As an example

An explanation of how to make three horizontal frames is as follows:

```
<html>

<head><title> Frames</title> </head>

<frameset rows = "20%,85%,20%"> <frame_name = "right" src = "www.google.com" /> <frame name = "About" src = "google.com" /> <frame_name = "top" src = "www.google.com" /> <noframes> <body>Frame is here </body> </no_frames> </frame_set> </html>
```

5.14 iframe

By using the HTML tag <iframe>, you can build an inline frame. The <iframe> tag isn't linked to the <frameset> tag in any way; instead, it may appear everywhere in your code. The <iframe> tag is in charge of identifying an oblong segment inside the document where the browser will view a different document, complete with scrollbars and borders. An iframe is used To insert one document in the other document.

5.16 Src

This attribute specifies the name of the file to be enabled in the frame. Any URL may be used as its value. Src = "www.google/top.htm" will, for example, open an HTML file from the HTML directory.

5.17 name

You may assign a frame a name with this attribute. It is used to specify the frame in which a text should be loaded. It is particularly useful when creating links in one frame that load websites in another frame since the second frame requires a name to mark itself as the link's destination.

5.18 frame border

This attribute determines whether or not the frame's boundaries are visible; whether one is specified, it takes precedence over the value specified and in-frame order attribute also on <frameset> name, which may take one of two values: 1 (yes) or 0 (no) (no).

5.19 margin width

This attribute helps define the area's base between the frame's boundaries and the substance on the left side. Pixels are used to express the value. For instance, margin width = "20."

5.20 margin height

This feature helps define the area's size between the frame's boundaries and its contents at the top and bottom. Pixels are used to express the value. For instance, margin height = "15" is a good example.

5.21 height

This attribute defines the height of an iframe.

5.22 scrolling

This attribute regulates the presence of the scrollbars on the frame. The accepts one of three values: "yes," "no," or "auto." Scrolling = "no" suggests that there should be no scroll bars.

5.23 <longdesc

You may use this attribute to include a path to another page that contains a detailed summary of the frame's contents. <longdesc = "frame.html" is an example.

5.24 width

This attribute defines the width of an iframe.

5.25 Advanced Features:

HTML is a pretty simple code to use, so much so that if people have a clear understanding, they leap right into creating web pages without considering much about HTML's basics.

As a result, most web developers are squandering their time and resources by not fully using HTML and CSS, rendering their lives more complicated.

The distinction between abstract and actual tags is among the most important basic principles in HTML that once grasped, can have a significant effect on a web designer's workflow.

Conclusion

My friends, this little book has already come to a close. While I hope that you will be able to use HTML "off the shelf" in your area, you will be satisfied if it merely sparks your curiosity. The approaches outlined in this book are among the most important ways for HTML users at all levels to improve their efficiency and proficiency. Consider if you and your teammates can and should utilize these – and other opportunities that will inevitably become available – to maximize performance. This book is intended for those who are new to the field. You also attempted to address the following topics in this book, which are equally essential for beginners and professionals:

- HTML for Beginners – all you need to talk about HTML in one location

- An overview of how HTML utilizes tags to identify the content of web pages

- Ideas on how to best design the template of your web pages

- Strategies for modifying the styles, fonts, and colors of elements

- A look into how you can connect with the web page users using forms and input boxes

- Examples of how to put what you've learned into practice when you create websites

- Formatting, scaling, fonts, graphics, gradients, multimedia, shapes, sprites, and – all the resources you need to customize your website fully!

CSS

For Beginners

The Best CSS Guide For Beginners To Learn Learn CSS in
One Day and Developing a Strong Coding Foundation

By

Ethan Hall

introduction
TO CSS
FOR
BEGINNERS

ICANBUILDABLOG.COM

Introduction

CSS was introduced by Hakom Lie in 1996 and collaborate by Bert Bos. Designed to be used in conjunction with HTML. CSS is used to style a web browser or HTML code. CSS specifies how HTML components should be rendered. Cascading Style Sheets is the programming language used to style web material.

Using CSS, we may adjust the presentation and style of the webpage. We may also specify how a website's appearance varies on various platforms, such as handheld devices, personal computers, and tablets. CSS is not a scripting language in the same way as JavaScript or C++ are. CSS, on the other hand, is also not as simple as it appears. You may have problems with web creation if you want to do it without learning. As a result, studying CSS is almost as useful as we learn a programming language. CSS greatly improves the graphic appearance of a website.

Chapter-1: What is CSS?

CSS is an abbreviation of Cascading Style Sheets. The focus is on "Style." It is just a style sheet language. It is not a mark-up language that is used to describe the appearance of a written text, such as HTML and is in charge of how the web pages will appear. CSS specifies how HTML items can appear on paper, screen, and in all other mediums. CSS is simple to learn and comprehend. CSS is most widely seen in conjunction with the scripting languages such as HTML as well as XHTML.

The fact that CSS cascades are a pretty cool function. Cascading implies that using certain guidelines, one or many style sheets may be added to an HTML document consecutively. This priority-cascading scheme is consistent. CSS helps you save time and effort. It has the ability to monitor the structure of several web pages at the same time. As a result, the same tag will have several types. For fifty pages of a website, a Web developer might choose to reduce the standard text size around 16pt to 12pt. If all of the pages have same style sheet, changing the text size on the style sheet would cause all of the pages to display the tiny text.

In brief, you could use it for styling HTML documents like page fonts, table sizes, layouts, and colors. Cascading Style Sheets CSS files store external stylesheets.

You can also make the most current design take precedence over previous styles. For instance, with CSS, we may specify that each of the text should be 14px high. We may even claim later that we like it to be blue in color. Later, we can make one sentence bold or that green should be used instead of blue color.

Although CSS is well known for designing text styles, but it can also be used to format other elements of a Web page's architecture. CSS may be used to describe picture padding, the thickness, design, and color of a border of the table and the padding of table cells and other items. CSS allows Web designers more precise command over the appearance of Web pages than HTML does. This is the reason that most modern Web sites use CSS.

You may also use the CSS language to apply effects or graphics to the website. It can be used to display CSS animations such as button click effects, animated backgrounds, spinners, and loaders.

Your website will look as a simple HTML page if you don't use CSS. If we disable Facebook's CSS, this is what it would look like:

Jump to
Sections of this page
Accessibility help
Press alt + / to open this menu

Facebook

Email or Phone   Password

[   ] [   ] [Log In]
                   Forgotten account?
Facebook helps you connect and share with the people in your life.

Create an account
It's quick and easy.
An error occurred. Please try again.
We couldn't create your account
We were not able to sign you up for Facebook.
[First name]
[Surname]
[Mobile number or email addr]
[Re-enter email address]
[New password]
Birthday
[14 ▼] [Jan ▼] [1995 ▼]
Gender
◯ Female ◯ Male ◯ Custom
[Select your pronoun   ▼]
Your pronoun is visible to everyone.
[Gender (optional)]

By clicking Sign Up, you agree to our Terms, Data Policy and Cookie Policy. You may receive SMS notifications from us and can opt out at any time.

1.1 CSS Versions

CSS1 (Level 1) was released as a suggestion by the World Wide Web Consortium (W3C) during 1996 in the month of December. This edition includes a basic visual styling model across every HTML tag, as well as a summary of the CSS language.

CSS2 is recommended by W3C that is constructed on CSS1 (Cascading Style Sheets, level 1) and was released in May 1998. Style sheets that are Media-specific, such as printers as well as element placement, downloadable fonts and tables, have been included in this edition.

1.2 Difference between HTML and CSS

HTML, or hypertext mark-up language, is used to create the majority of websites. This is the most popular way to add color, fonts, hyperlinks (clickable text which takes the user elsewhere), and graphic doodads. However, the size of the websites can increase. When this occurs, HTML becomes very difficult to perform a very simple task. Cascading style sheets can create web site's design simple once more!

Consider CSS to be a dress code for computers. CSS is mostly used to illustrate how web pages can appear. Much better, Cascading style sheets can be conveniently removed from HTML, making it easier to locate the dress code. It updates the appearance of your website quickly and can edit it easily. You should adjust your CSS, much as a uniform at school, and your student's appearance can change as well. Style sheets encourage you to quickly update whole websites if you want, similar to how a fashionista encourages people to evolve with time whilst also being the same individuals. CSS can make the website more colorful, nicer, and clearer, while HTML merely creates the foundation or the skeleton.

1.3 Difference between HTML and CSS

It is briefly explained here:

S.NO.	HTML	CSS
1.	HTML stands for **H**yper **T**ext **M**arkup **L**anguage.	CSS stands for **C**ascading **S**tyle **S**heets.
2.	It is a basic mark-up language.	It is an extension of HTML
3.	It is used to describe the layout of a web page.	It is used to style web pages by utilizing various styling features.
4.	HTML consists of tags in which text is enclosed.	CSS consists of declaration and selectors blocks.
5.	Visualization and presentation can not be done by HTML.	Visualization and presentation can be done by CSS.
6.	It has less support and backup.	It has higher support and backup.
7.	HTML can not be used inside a CSS sheet.	CSS can be used inside an HTML document.
8.	HTML doesn't have any types.	CSS has two types: internal or external which depending on the requirement.

Html Example

```html
<html>
<body>
    <h1>This is an HTML example</h1>
</body>
</html>
```

Output:

This is a HTML example

CSS Example

```html
<html>
<head>
<style>
body {
background-color:orange;
}
</style>
</head>
<body>

<h1>This is a CSS example</h1>

<p>This page has orange background color</p>

</body>
</html>
```

Output:

This is a CSS example

This page has orange background color

1.4 Advantages of CSS

Following are the advantages of the CSS:

- CSS saves you time by allowing you to write CSS once and reuse it through several pages.
- Cascading sheets simplify website creation and management by affecting the entire website with a single line of code update.
- CSS provides a wider variety of features and better styles than HTML.
- Since there is fewer coding on the page, it takes less time for it to load.
- Compatibility for a variety of devices.
- Uses an offline cache to allow for offline surfing.
- The script ensures platform independence as well as it is compatible with the most recent browsers.
- HTML attributes still are frowned upon, and it is recommended that all HTML sites use Cascading Style Sheet to ensure compatibility with potential browsers.
- The user can easily modify the online web page.
- Since it is less complicated, the work required is greatly decreased.

- It decreases the size of a transferring file.
- To improve site speed, web designers can use a few lines of code for each website.

1.5 Disadvantages of CSS

Following are the disadvantages of the CSS:

- When it comes to CSS, what fit's in one browser may not fit in another. The web developers could verify the program's consistency by running it in different browsers.
- If any incompatibilities arise after making the modifications, we must check the consistency. All browsers are affected by the same change.
- CSS, especially CSS 1 to CSS 3, causes web browsers to become confused.
- Different browsers handle CSS in different ways. CSS is supported differently in Internet Explorer and Opera.

1.6 Importance of CSS

Web pages were severely limited in function and appearance prior to the W3C development of CSS in 1996. A website was shown as plain images, text, hypertext, and links to many other hyperlinks sites in early browsers. There was no style at all, just a simple column of paragraphs running around the paper.

CSS enabled web designers to do things like:

- specify new fonts besides the browser's default fonts
- specify colors and size of links and text
- add colors to the backgrounds
- include webpage elements into boxes and move certain boxes to unique locations on the website

They added "style" to style sheets, allowing for the very first time the design of Web pages.

W3C was the initial commercial browser that interprets and use CSS in 1998. Support for such CSS functions varies from website to website to this day. The W3C, which continues to oversee and develop Web standards, just published a new CSS and CSS3 standard. Developers of CSS3 expect that all web browsers can interpret and view all CSS functions in the same manner.

1.7 WHY should everyone learn CSS?

There is a number of websites who offer free or low-cost templates, but even that restricts how much we can develop and leaves us with a site that resembles just like everyone else's. The most popular websites are those that stick out, are entertaining, and unforgettable in their representation of your brand. We want to attract the consumers to make an order, recommend a friend to our services, or become regular customers. We risk getting overlooked if our page mixes with the audience.

Knowing how to create our website with Hypertext Markup Language, CSS allows us to look unique from the audience with a genuine, hand-crafted illustration of our company or any major company. Saving money on any potential websites we may like to build and create good websites with CSS and HTML.

1.8   How can CSS help you?

Cascading Style Sheets can help you in many ways. Some of them are mentioned below:

i.   **Important for web designers**

CSS is a useful method of controlling the appearance of web pages. Text, fonts, colors, borders, design and backgrounds are all controlled by CSS. CSS has a number of major benefits over other web design methods.

ii. Redesign Website Quickly

It's challenging to redesign several older websites which were designed without CSS. However, if a site is created with CSS, it can easily be revamped. Backgrounds and colors can change the appearance of a website with little effort. Now, many sites make special editions of their websites for special events, and they may take less time to create an alternative style sheet.

iii. Change Website Designs

It's simple to create a website using a free Web design. However, these designs are rarely elegant, so your website would resemble any other online website. You may change these designs using CSS to show your styles and colors. As a result, you'll get a personalized website without putting in a lot of work.

iv. To Earn Money

You can offer these facilities to other websites once you've mastered CSS. And if you want to work as a freelance or independent web designer, you won't succeed much unless you know CSS.

v. To Save Money

There are several web designers that can create your CSS or website for you. However, even though you just pay them to create the designs and you manage the content, hiring someone else may be costly. When you encounter minor bugs that you can solve yourself, understanding how to update the CSS can save you money. You'll be capable of solving larger and more challenging issues when you practice.

vi.   Build Diverse Websites

CSS allows pages to appear very distinct from one website to the next without requiring a lot of code. Some websites, for example, now use subtle color differences across various parts of the web pages. You may use page IDs to modify the Cascading Style Sheet for each segment while keeping the same HTML layout. The content and CSS are the only things that alter.

1.9 Is CSS worth it?

HTML and CSS are definitely worth learning. CSS is an interesting language because, although it's fundamentals are easy, it is immensely complex and allows you full access to the world's most efficient rendering engine: the browser.

You can use the rendering engine to generate documents and apps on every device on earth. Browsers and the internet are not only the greatest way to deliver software to billions of people around the globe, but they also provide you access to the native innovation world.

Native mobile apps have browsers such as CSS, HTML, and JavaScript, which is the most famous development framework for native mobile apps. Electron, which allows you to package CSS, HTML, and JavaScript for the desktop, is used to create desktop applications like Skype, Slack, Atom, and many more. CSS gives you access to the whole world.

Chapter-2: Basic of CSS

Let's learn some basics of the Cascading Style Sheets.

2.1 How does CSS work?

To grasp the fundamentals of CSS, you should first grasp a clear understanding of modern HTML. The "box model" is used by web designers to set out web pages. A Web page is made up of a collection of boxes, each of which contains a distinct feature. The boxes are clustered, meaning they are one within the other.

A page's header, for example, is just a box that includes many smaller boxes that include many of the elements that make a header, such as a logo, navigation, shopping cart buttons, and so on. A developer adds different styles to a "header" box using CSS. Let's imagine that the developer renders the text within the header purple, which has Arial font and is fifteen points bigger in this case.

The "cascading" aspect of CSS falls into action here. The font types used in the header are applied across all of the items inside the header. Elements like navigation, links, and calls to action would all be in purple color, Arial, and fifteen points bigger.

2.2 Implementation of CSS code in HTML

You may also be thinking that how this Cascading Style Sheet coding is implemented to HTML text. CSS is written in plain text using a word processor or text editor on your device, similar to HTML. There are three ways to use CSS in HTML documents:

- Inline CSS
- Internal CSS

- External CSS

Note: In external Cascading Style Sheets, we have the styles, which is a very popular way to implement CSS. But you may also use Inline CSS and Internal CSS depending on your needs.

2.2.1 Inline CSS

An inline Cascading Style Sheets is used to give a distinctive style to a particular HTML element, which is located in the body section. The style attribute is used to specify this type of style inside an HTML tag. You won't need to use selectors for that kind of CSS design because you'll just need to apply a style attribute into every HTML tag. As a result, Inline CSS appears right next to the component it picks.

This CSS form is not suggested since every HTML tag must be styled separately. Only if you are using inline CSS, handling your website can become too difficult. Inline Cascading Style Sheets in HTML, on the other hand, maybe helpful in certain cases. For instance, if you can't access the CSS files and you just need to add styles to a particular element.

Example

Consider the following example. We apply inline CSS to <p> and <h1> tags here:

```
<!DOCTYPE html>
<html>
<body style="background-color:black;">
<h1 style="color:white;padding:30px;">Applying inline CSS</h1>
<p style="color:white;">This is an Inline example.</p>
</body>
</html>
```

Output:

Example 2

```html
<!DOCTYPE html>
<html>
<body style="background-color:black;">
<h1  style="font-size:40px;color:violet;">Watch this headline</h1>
<p style="color:white;">This is an Inline example.</p>
</body>
</html>
```

Output:

Example Explained

<h1 style="font-size:40px;color:violet;">Watch this headline</h1>

Above line of code would cause one specific headline on a single .html page to appear in violet, 40 point font.

Benefits of Inline CSS

Benefits of the inline CSS are as under:

- Adding Cascading Style Sheets rules to the HTML page is simple and convenient. As a result, this method is suitable for previewing or testing the modifications to the website as well as making fast fixes.
- As opposed to the external format, you do not need to develop and upload documents separately.

Drawbacks of Inline CSS

Drawbacks of the inline CSS are as under:

- Adding Cascading Style Sheets rules to each HTML element takes time and leaves the HTML layout unorganized.

- Styling various elements will influence the size and duration of downloading your website.

2.2.2 Internal CSS

Internal CSS is also defined as Embedded Cascading Style Sheets because it's used to add a style to a single HTML page.

Internal CSS is specified in the <head> portion of a Hyper Text Markup Language (HTML) page, inside <style>...</style> i.e., the CSS is located inside an HTML file.

Internal Cascading Style Sheets are typically used when the entire page has a single specific design for each component. Moreover, using this design for different sites takes time since CSS rules must be added to each page on the website.

Example

```
<!DOCTYPE html>
<html>
<head>
<style>
body {background-color: powderblue;}
h1   {color: blue;}
p    {color: red;}
</style>
</head>
<body>

<h1>This is a heading in blue color</h1>
<p>This is a paragraph in red color.</p>

</body>
```

```
</html>
```

Output:

This is a heading in blue color

This is a paragraph in red color.

Benefits of Internal CSS

Benefits of the internal CSS are as under:

- Using the same style on different sites takes time, so CSS rules must be added to each page on the website.
- In this style sheet, you can apply ID and class selectors.

Example

```
.class {
    property1 : value1;
    property2 : value2;
    property3 : value3;
}

#id {
    property1 : value1;
    property2 : value2;
    property3 : value3;
}
```

Drawbacks of Internal CSS

The drawback of the internal CSS is:

- Applying the code into an HTML document will make the page size larger and take longer to load.

2.2.3 External CSS

For certain HTML pages, an external CSS is applied to describe the style. External CSS is a separate CSS file that only contains style property through tag attributes (for example, class, id, heading, and so on). CSS properties can be written in a different file with the .css extension that can be generated using a text editor of any type on your monitor (for example, Notepad++) and can be added to the HyperText Markup Language (HTML) document by using the link tag. This CSS approach is more effective, especially when styling a huge website. You can modify the whole site by modifying a single.css file.

By using an external CSS, you must have the header section in the .html files that connects to external CSS which appears like this:

```
<head>
<link rel="stylesheet" type="text/css" href=mysitestyle.css">
</head>
```

This would connect a .html file with the external CSS, and all the CSS commands within the file will be applied to the .html pages connected to it.

Example

Attach a link to an external CSS in to the <head> portion of every HTML page to use it:

```
<!DOCTYPE html>
<html>
<head>
  <link rel="stylesheet" href="styles.css">
```

```
</head>
<body>

<h1>This is a heading in blue color</h1>
<p>This is a paragraph in red color.</p>

</body>
</html>
```

Output:

This is a heading in blue color

This is a paragraph in red color.

Any text editor can be used to create the external CSS. The file should be saved with the .css extension and should not have any HTML code.

Here is how the "styles.css" file will look like:

"styles.css":
```
body {
  background-color: powderblue;
}
h1 {
color: blue;
}
p {
```

```
 color: red;
}
```

Benefits of External CSS

The benefits of the external CSS are as under:

- The HTML files would have a clearer layout because the CSS coding is located in a different document.
- The coding is easy to manage.
- It decreases the amount of code in half.
- Rather than making adjustments to several HTML files, we may make changes to only one file.
- Multiple pages make use of the same .css doc/files.

Drawbacks of External CSS

Drawbacks of the external CSS are as under:

- Once the external style sheet is loaded, the pages can not work correctly.
- Linking or uploading to several CSS files will extend the time it takes for your site to load.

To use External CSS

For using external CSS, follow these steps:

1. Using the text editor, make a new .css document and apply the style rules.

2. After the <title> tag, in <head> portion of a HTML sheet, add a link to the external .css file.

Remember to replace style.css and name it as your own .css file.

External CSS is a most effective way to implement Cascading Style Sheets on the website (it's easy to be aware of and create a website's style from the specific CSS file), whereas inline style and internal CSS could be used on a particular instance where individual style improvements are required.

2.3 Syntax

CSS syntax is made up of a series of rules. CSS syntax is divided into three sections:

- Selectors
- Declaration
- Property

2.3.1 Selectors

This is the name of the HTML component at the beginning of the ruleset. It specifies the styled element(s). To put it another way, a Selector will be any tag to which you choose to apply styles. Modify the selector to style a new element. Selectors include h1 to h6, id, p, class, and others.

2.3.2 Declaration

The CSS language's core feature is to set CSS properties to unique values. A declaration is a value and property pair, and every CSS engine determines which declarations refer to each and every element on a page in order to properly layout and style it.

A colon separates the name and value of the CSS property that includes in each declaration. For Example:

It is one rule, like color: blue;. It defines which property of an element you would like to style. Declaration block is enclosed by curly braces and includes one or multiple declarations divided by semicolons.

One or multiple property-value pairs make up the declaration block.

2.3.3 Property

The property is an identifier that can be a name that specifies which attribute is taken into account.

The HTML element may be styled in a variety of ways. In Cascading Style Sheets, you can choose the properties you want the rule to affect.

Property value

Property value is declared just after the colon on the right side of the property. This selects out of the several potential appearances for a specific needed property from a large number of options. A collection of valid values exists for each property. CSS is case-insensitive by nature with all properties and values.

Example

All <p> components in this example will be center-aligned and have a red text color:

```
p {
  color: red;
  text-align: center;
}
```

Output:

Hello World!

These paragraphs are styled with CSS.

Example Explained

- p is a CSS selector (it refers to the HTML attribute <p> that you need to style).
- In this property is color, and property value is red.
- Same in this case, the property is text-align, and the property value is center.

CSS Syntax

CSS has several syntaxes, such as the standard syntax, which is straightforward but does not provide much help.

You have to be familiar with the following syntax:

- Color syntax
- Margin Syntax
- White space syntax
- The syntax for CSS pseudo-classes
- Pseudo-element syntax
- Attribute selector syntax
- Background-color syntax
- Borders syntax
- Padding syntax
- Height and width syntax
- Fonts syntax
- The syntax for links, tables, lists.

2.4 Ruleset

A ruleset is a name given to the whole framework. In layman's terms, it's a series of laws. A law, also known as a "ruleset," is a declaration that instructs browsers on how to display certain elements over an HTML page. One or more comma separates every declaration block that are conditions that select certain elements of the web page. A ruleset, or rule, is made up of a selector group and a related declarations block. In the illustration below, a Cascading Style Sheets rule is depicted:

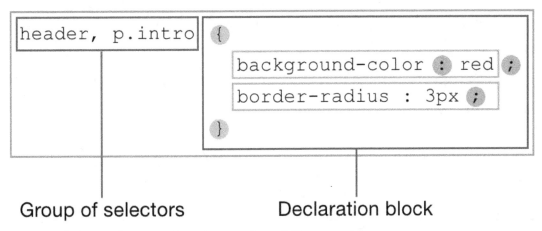

<table>
<tr><td>Group of selectors</td><td>Declaration block</td></tr>
</table>

Group of selectors   **Declaration block**

Take note of the other main elements of the syntax:

- Each ruleset, with the exception of the selector, must be enclosed in curly braces. ({})
- Use a colon (:) to distinguish the property with it's values inside each declaration.
- Each declaration must be separated from each other by a semicolon (;) inside each ruleset.

Example

To change several property values inside a single ruleset, use semicolons to divide them, as in:

```
p {
  color: red;
  width: 500px;
  border: 1px solid black;
}
```

Breaking it down:

- Everything here is a set of rules (ruleset).
- Everything within these curly braces is the declaration block.
- A selector is a little part before the starting curly brace.

- A declaration is a key or value pair divided by the colon and terminating in a semicolon.
- Property (property name) is a key, and value (property value) is a value in these value keys or pairs.

2.5 Selectors Types

Let's discuss some types of selectors.

2.5.1 Simple selectors

CSS has a few basic selectors for selecting elements:

- Element Selector
- id Selector
- Class Selector

Element Selector

It uses the element name to pick HTML elements. Type selector or a tag is another name for it.

Example

On this page, all <p> elements have a blue text color and have center-alignment:

```
p {
  text-align: center;
  color: blue;
}
```

Output:

Every paragraph will be affected by the style.

Me too!

And me!

id Selector

The id attribute is used to select an element that is based on it's (id attribute's) value. Since the element's id is unique inside a page, the id selector can often use to pick only one specific element. Write # (hash) character preceded by the element's id to pick an element having a unique id.

Syntax

#idname

Example

The following CSS rule will be added to an HTML element having the id="para1" attribute.

```
#para1 {
  text-align: center;
  color: Green;
}
```

Output:

Hello World!

This paragraph is not affected by the style.

Note: A number cannot be the first character in the ID name.

Class Selector

The class selector is used to selecting the HTML elements that have a certain class attribute.

Type a period (.), accompanied by the name of a class so that we can select elements that have a particular class.

Syntax

.classname

Example

Every HTML element that have class="center" will be center-aligned and red in this case:

```
.center {
 text-align: center;
  color: red;
}
```

Output:

Red and center-aligned heading

Red and center-aligned paragraph.

Note: You might even decide that a class can have an impact on a particular HTML element.

Example 2

In the following example, only the <p> elements having the class="center" would be center-aligned and red.

```
p.center {
 text-align: center;
  color: red;
}
```

Output:

This heading will not be affected

This paragraph will be red and center-aligned.

Note: HTML elements may also be used to apply to several classes.

2.5.2 More Selectors

A few more selectors are as follow:

- Combinator selectors
- Pseudo-elements selectors
- Pseudo-class selectors
- Attribute selectors

Combinator selectors

It selects elements that are based on their unique relationship, while selectors in Cascading Style Sheets are used to style the content. A Cascading Style Sheets selector could be either basic or complicated, consisting of several selectors linked together by combinators. We may, for example, target just child elements from a parent element or an element that is accompanied by another element that has the same degree.

In CSS, it has four types:

- descendant selector (space)
- child selector (>)
- adjacent sibling selector (+)
- general sibling selector (~)

Pseudo-elements selectors

It's a keyword that you may apply to a selector to style a certain part of a selected element(s). Even so, instead of adding a class to current elements, they behave as though you had applied a completely new HTML feature to the mark-up. A double colon precedes pseudo-elements (::).

Syntax

It's syntax is:

```
selector::pseudo-element {
  property: value;
}
```

It may, for example, be used to:

- Style an element's first word or line.
- Add content before or after an element's content.

Example

::first-line, for example, is used to modify the font of a paragraph's first line.

```
p::first-line {
  color: blue;
  text-transform: uppercase;
}
```

Note: In the beginning, only one colon was used for pseudo-elements, so you could see it sometimes in earlier examples or codes. For the backward compatibility, modern browsers use the old pseudo-elements of single or double colon syntax.

Pseudo-class selectors

It's a keyword that is applied to the selector to pick elements that are based on a specific state. They behave as though you had added a class to a section of a document, resulting in more versatile, manageable code and, in many cases, reducing the number of classes in a mark-up. There are numerous other pseudo-classes to choose from. Keywords that begin with a colon are known as pseudo-classes.

For Example, it's uses are:

- It is used to style differently to the visited and unvisited links
- It style's an element when it is hovered over by a mouse pointer
- It style's an element when it is focused

Syntax

It's syntax is:

selector:pseudo-class {

  property: value;

}

For example, when the user's cursor hovers over a button, :hover can change it's color.

button:hover {

  color: blue;

}

Attribute selectors

It is used to choose an element that has a particular attribute value or attribute. The Attribute selector pairs items depending on whether or not they have a specific attribute. Attribute selectors are a simple and efficient way to add styles to HTML elements depending on the existence of a certain attribute value or attribute. By default, they are case-sensitive and enclosed in brackets [].

All of the <a> elements that have target attribute are selected in the following example:

Example

a[target] {

 background-color: yellow;

}

Output:

CSS [attribute] Selector

The links with a target attribute gets a yellow background:

w3schools.com disney.com wikipedia.org

Chapter 3: CSS Box Model

It's only normal to want more power over the functionality and design of your WordPress site while you run it yourself. CSS is one of the most useful ways for changing the appearance of a website. With CSS knowledge, you can alter anything from the layout of the page to the colors, fonts, and background images.

The CSS box model is among the most fundamental principles to learn all of this. It's a basic web design principle. Understanding it allows you to quite endlessly modify the style of your website to your liking.

To use CSS effectively, you must first know that everything on a website page is comprised of rectangles. Rectangular boxes are stacked parallel on top of, to, underneath, and enclosed inside each other on every website you visit.

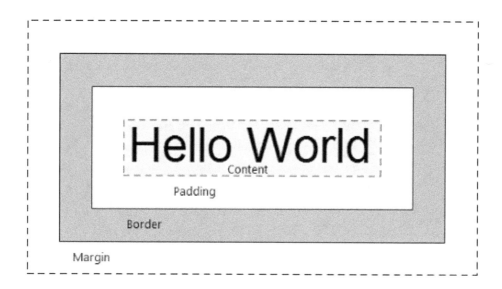

3.1 What exactly is a box model?

When discussing about layout and design in CSS, the expression "box model" is often used. The CSS box model is a box which wraps around any HTML element that has content, height and width. We can use it as a set of tools for personalizing the design of various elements or aligning them with one another. This involves adjusting the size, color, and position of the settings. The box model helps one to create space between elements and adds a border around them. This box is made up of several levels, so you can control it separately using CSS. This enables you to organize elements in various ways in comparison to each other and apply styles to them in a variety of ways.

Example

The box model is shown as follows:

```
div {
  width: 300px;
  border: 15px
solid green;
padding: 50px;
 margin: 20px;
}
```

Output:

Demonstrating the Box Model

The CSS box model is essentially a box that wraps around every HTML element. It consists of: borders, padding, margins, and the actual content.

This text is the content of the box. We have added a 50px padding, 20px margin and a 15px green border. Ut enim ad minim veniam, quis nostrud exercitation ullamco laboris nisi ut aliquip ex ea commodo consequat. Duis aute irure dolor in reprehenderit in voluptate velit esse cillum dolore eu fugiat nulla pariatur. Excepteur sint occaecat cupidatat non proident, sunt in culpa qui officia deserunt mollit anim id est laborum.

3.2 Box Model Properties

It's properties are:

- Content Area
- Width
- Height
- Padding
- Borders
- Margins

Note: The other properties, with the exception of width and height, are optional. That means we can also have a box without a border, padding, or margin.

The below diagram makes it easier for you to understand:

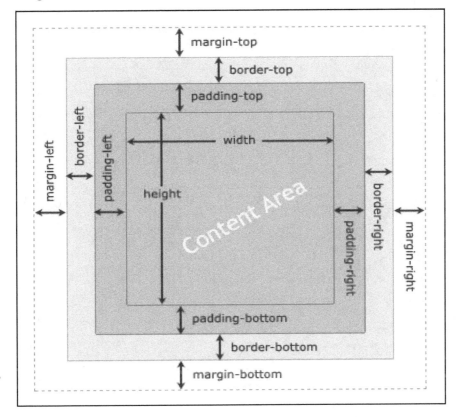

3.2.1 Content Area

This section contains content such as images, text, and other media. The content edge defines it's boundaries, and the height and width of the content box determine it's dimensions. It has some properties added to it.

3.2.2 Width

It is the width of an element's content area. This is set to 100% by default for the block elements. Inline elements may take up as much room as their content requires. It can have a value of auto, percentage, or length. When you use CSS to set the width of the element, you're really setting the width of a content area. Padding, boundaries, and margins must all be added when calculating the whole size of the element.

Example

The total width is 350px for this <div>:

```
div {
 width: 320px;
 padding: 10px;
 border: 5px solid                                        gray;
 margin: 0;
}
```

Output:

Calculate the total width:

The picture above is 350px wide. The total width of this element is also 350px.

An element's total width must be calculated as follows:

Total width = width + left padding + right padding + left border + right border + left margin + right margin

So,

320px (width)

+ 20px (left + right padding)

+ 10px (left + right border)

+ 0px (left + right margin)

= 350px

Values

It's values are:

auto

This is the default setting. The height and width are calculated by the browser.

length

It defines height and width in pixels, centimeters, and other terms.

%

It defines the width and height of the containing block in percent.

initial

 It sets height and width to their default values.

inherit

In this, the parent's height and width would be inherited.

3.2.3 Height

As you would expect, this indicates the height of an element. It is normally regulated by the data inside it, but if necessary, you may also set a certain height. Again, this is only applicable to block elements.

Example

Let's set the height and width of <div> element:

```
div {
 height: 100px;
  width: 500px;
  background-color: powderblue;
}
```

Output:

Set the height and width of an element

This div element has a height of 100px and a width of 500px.

An element's total height must be calculated as follows:

Total element height = height + top padding + bottom padding + top border + bottom border + top margin + bottom margin

So,

100px (height)

+ 20px (left + right padding)

+ 10px (left + right border)

+ 0px (left + right margin)

= 130px

Values

It's values are same as width's values.

3.2.4 Padding

This area is the space between the content area and the boundary box. Padding is a transparent layer. It's the space that surrounds a paragraph text. The width and height of a padding-box determine it's dimensions. This is essential, for example, to keep text inside of the HTML element to make it readable.

CSS padding may be changed to accomplish the following effects:

Increase the amount of space between the content and the border

It is a very popular utilization of padding, and it is very useful for adding whitespace within elements.

Alter the size of the Element

Content will have exactly the same size as before, but there will be more room around it when you rise padding value. When you try to extend the clickable region with digital elements like buttons, this is handy.

Adding some Padding

When looking at this example, the most noticeable features that we notice is the text which is directly bordering on the element's side. It causes it difficult to read and unappealing to the eyes. Fortunately, the padding clause allows us to change this. For **Example**

```
example-element {
background-color: deepskyblue;
border: 15px solid blue;
height: 300px;
padding: 16px;
width: 300px;
}
```

And the result is:

Lorem ipsum dolor sit amet, consectetur
adipiscing elit.

Keep in mind that, just as with the border, various padding values can be set
on different corners/sides of the element. To do this, use padding: top;,
padding: right;, padding: bottom; and padding: left;.

You may also use padding: 15px 8px 25px 5px; as a shorthand property. It
shows the padding on the top, right, bottom, and left sides.

Padding is among the only few properties in this list which can be used on inline elements as well. However, be aware that the bottom and top padding can encroach on other elements, so bear that in mind.

Padding values

Lengths, percentages, and inherit are used to set padding values. It is incapable of accepting negative values. For every padding property, the original or default value is 0.

length

It specifies the padding in pt, px, cm, and other terms.

%

It specifies the padding in percent of the underlying element's width.

inherit

It specifies that padding of the child element must be inherited.

Padding of every side of the element could be defined using CSS properties:

- padding-top
- padding-right
- padding-bottom
- padding-left

Shorthand Property

It is feasible to write all padding properties inside one property to simplify the code.

It is be used for:

- padding-top
- padding-right
- padding-bottom
- padding-left

Syntax

top padding, right padding, bottom padding and left padding.

It works like this:

padding: [top] [left] [right] [bottom];

For Example

padding: 25px 50px 75px 100px;

- top padding is 25px
- right padding is 50px
- bottom padding is 75px
- left padding is 100px

Example

Shorthand property which has four values, can be shown as:

div {

 padding: 25px 50px 75px 100px;

}

Output:

The padding shorthand property - 4 values

This div element has a top padding of 25px, a right padding of 50px, a bottom padding of 75px, and a left padding of 100px.

Longhand Property

Longhand can be used to declare all padding properties individually. As a result, the above example can be re-written as:

div {

 padding-top: 25px;

 padding-right: 50px;

 padding-bottom: 75px;

```
    padding-left: 100px;

}
```

3.2.5 Margin

Finally, the term "margin" refers to the area outside the border. It is essential for page architecture, alignment, and spacing since it essentially manages the gap between various elements. Around the box, the margin is opaque. The margin-box width and height are the dimensions of the Margin area. It is beneficial to separate an element from it's neighbouring elements. Other items are moved out of the box. Margin values can be positive or negative. When you use a negative margin solely on a single side of the box, it can overlap other elements on the webpage. We may use the margin property to manage all of the element's margins at once or the corresponding longhand properties to control either side individually:

- margin-top
- margin-right
- margin-bottom
- margin-left

Basic Syntax

top-margin, right margin, a bottom margin, and left margin.

For-Example

margin: 16px 25px 30px 16px;

The top margin is 16 pixels, the right margin is 25 pixels, the bottom margin is 35 pixels, and the left margin is 16 pixels.

Margin property can define one to four values. That value is either a <length>, <percentage>, or the auto keyword.

- If only one value is defined, the same margin is applied on all four sides.

- Where two values are defined, the top and bottom margins need to apply first, followed by the left and right margins.
- Where three values are defined, the first margin is applied on top, the second on the right and left, and the third to bottom.
  - When four values are defined, the margins are applied in a clockwise direction.

Values

It's values are as follow:

length

It sets the margin's size as a constant value.

percentage

The margin's size is defined as a percentage.

auto

The browser chooses an appropriate margin to apply. This value, for example, may be used to focus an element in certain situations.

Margin Example

Set various margins on each of the <p> element's four sides:

```
p {
  margin-top: 100px;
  margin-bottom: 100px;
  margin-right: 150px;
  margin-left: 80px;
}
```

Output:

Using individual margin properties

This div element has a top margin of 100px, a right margin of 150px, a bottom margin of 100px, and a left margin of 80px.

Shorthand Syntax

margin: unit's|initial|inherit|auto;

Where unit's will use values in px, em, length, percent, and so on.

This syntax simultaneously sets values as margin-top, margin-bottom, margin-right, and margin-left.

Example

```
<style>
  .margin_shorthand1 {
    border:20px solid powderblue;
    margin: 5px;
}
  .margin_shorthand2 {
    border:15px solid orange;
    margin: 20px 10px;
}
.margin_shorthand3 {
    border:8px solid pink;
    margin: 30px 10px 20px;
```

```
}
  .margin_shorthand4 {
     border:12px solid aqua;
     margin: 0 15px 20px 5px;
  }
}
</style>
```

Output:

If margin has 1 value

> **margin: 5px;** means: margin-top:5px;margin-right:5px;margin-bottom:5px;margin-left:5px;

If margin has 2 values

> **margin: 20px 10px;** means: margin-top:20px;margin-right:10px;margin-bottom:20px;margin-left:10px;

If margin has 3 values

> **margin: 30px 10px 20px;** means: margin-top:30px;margin-right:10px;margin-bottom:20px;margin-left:10px;

If it's value is one.

For Example

margin: 10px;

then, the top, right, bottom, and the left margin is 10px each.

If it's value is two.

For Example

margin: 0.5em 1em;

then, 0.5em is set for the top and bottom margins each, while the right and left margins are 1em each.

If it's value is three.

For Example

margin: 5px 3px 8px;

then, the top margin is 5px, the right and left margins are 3px each, and the bottom margin is 8px.

If it's value is four.

For Example

margin: 10px 2em 15px 5px;

then, the top margin is 10px, the right margin is 2em, the bottom margin is 15px, and the left margin is 5px.

Margin collapsing

The idea of margin collapse is crucial to grasp when it comes to margins. If the margins of two elements touch and both are positive, the margins will merge to form a single margin, that is, the length of the biggest individual margin. When the margin is negative for one or two margins, the total will subtract the negative value.

There are two paragraphs in the below example. Top paragraph's bottom margin is 50-pixel. Top margin of the second paragraph is 30 pixels. Since margins have merged, the real margin between these boxes is 50 pixels, rather than the sum of both margins.

There are few rules that govern when margins collapse and when it does not. For the time being, the most important factor to note is that margin collapse is a real thing. This is most likely what is occurring when you use margins to create space and don't have the space you want.

3.2.6 Border

It's the straight line right outside padding and right in the middle of the margin. They come in a variety of designs, colors, and sizes. Strong, dotted, double, dashed, ridge, groove, inset, outset, or zero are all options. If desired, it can even have rounded corners. The important thing to note is that a border sit's between the padding and margin of the element, and it's usually opaque to cover some background color. The border couldn't be used to set customized value for the border-image; however, it sets itself to it's default value, which is none. The width and height of the border determine it's dimensions. The short hand border-width and border properties define the density of borders. When box-sizing property is assigned to the border-box, the height, max-height, min-height, width, max-width, and min-width properties may be used to specify the size of the border region.

Short hand border

Border property in CSS is the shorthand syntax that accepts several values to draw one line across the element. Any excluded sub-values would be set to it's original value, like all shorthand properties.

When you need all of the boundaries to look the same, the border shorthand comes in handy. Longhand border-style, border-color and border-width properties, which acknowledge different values on each line, can be used to differentiate them. You can also use the (border-top and border-block-start) properties of the border to aim single border at one time.

Syntax

top-border, right border, bottom border, and left border.

Example

.box {
  border: 3px solid red;
  height: 200px;
  width: 200px;
}

Value

One or many of the preceding values can be used in combination with boundary property. It makes no difference what order the values are in. If the border's style isn't defined, it would be invisible. This happened because it's style is set to none by default.

It's values are:

- border-style
- border-color
- border-width

border-style

It sets the border's style. If nothing is specified, the value defaults to none.

border-color

The color of a border is set here. If no color is specified, the default color is used.

border-width

The width of a border is set here. If no value is specified, it defaults to medium.

styling borders

In CSS, there are several properties to choose from when it comes to border styling. There are only four borders, each with a different style, color and width that we can change. Border property allows you to change the style, width and color of every border in one go.

You may use the following commands to customize the properties of every side individually:

- border-top
- border-left
- border-right

- border-bottom

You may use the most detailed longhand properties to change the width, color and style of one side:

- border-top-color
- border-top-style
- border-top-width
- border-right-color
- border-right-style
- border-right-width
- border-bottom-color
- border-bottom-style
- border-bottom-width
- border-left-color
- border-left-style
- border-left-width

Using the following to set color, width and style on each side:

- border-color
- border-width
- border-style

border-color

The color of the four borders is set by this property. The value of this property can range from one to four.

The color can be adjusted using the following methods:

- **name**

    specifying it by the name of the colors, such as "blue"

- **RGB**

    Specifying it by RGB values, such as "rgb(266,0,1)"

- **HSL**

    Specifying it by HSL values, such as "hsl(0, 50%, 100%)"
- **HEX**

    Specifying it by HEX values, such as "#ff0010"
- **transparent**

Note: When border-color isn't defined, the element's color is used. Border-style property must always be set prior to the border-color property. Before you can alter the color of an element, it should have borders.

If border-color property consists of four values:

border-color: green pink blue red;

- top border is green
- right border is pink
- bottom border is blue
- left border is red

If border-color property consists of three values:

border-color: blue red green;

- top border is blue
- right and left borders are red
- bottom border is green

If border-color property consists of two values:

border-color: green red;
- top and bottom borders are green
- right and left borders are red

If border-color property consists of one value:

border-color: blue;

- all four borders are blue

Example 1

Let's add color to all borders:

```
p {
 border-style: solid;
 border-color: #ff0000                                    #0000ff;
}
```

Output:

One-colored border!

Example 2

```
p.one {
  border-style: solid;
  border-color: red            green            blue            yellow;
}
```

Output:

The border-color Property

The border-color property can have from one to four values (for the top border, right border, bottom border, and the left border):

A solid multicolor border

Border width

Border-width property determines how wide the borders of an element should be. The value of this property will range between one to four.

Examples

border-width: medium thin 10px thick;

- top border is medium
- right border is thin
- bottom border is 10px
- left border is thick

border-width: medium thick thin;

- top border is medium
- right and left borders are thick
- bottom border is thin

border-width: medium thin;

- top and bottom borders are medium
- right and left borders are thin

border-width: thick;

- all four borders are thick

Note: Border-style property should always be declared prior to border-width property. Before you set a width of an element, it must have some borders.

Example

Now let's set borders width:

div {border-width: thin;}

Output:

A heading with a thin border

A div element with a thin border.

Note: The border-width property does not work if it is used alone. Use the border-style property to set the border first.

3.3 Types of Box Model

There are two types of the box model. These are as under:

3.3.1 Standard box model

When you assign a box, it's width and hight attribute in this model type, the content box's height and width are specified. The height and width of the box are then applied to random border and padding to have the overall size taken by that box. Browsers already use the same box model by default.

Example

Suppose that the box's height, width, margin, padding and border are all specified by CSS:

```
.box {
  width: 350px;
  height: 150px;
  margin: 10px;
  padding: 25px;
  border: 5px solid black;
}
```

Output:

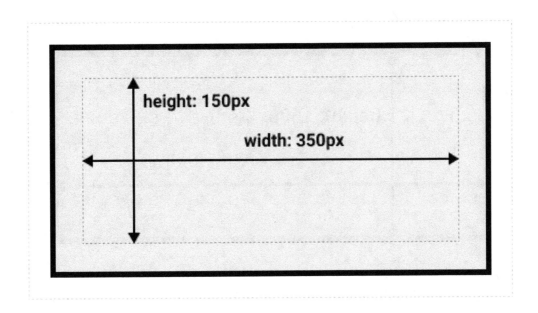

In above standard box model, the space occupied by the box would eventually be 410px (350 + 25 + 25 + 5 + 5), and it's height is 210px (150 + 25 + 25 + 5 + 5), since the border and padding was attached to the content box's width used by content box.

3.3.2 Alternative box model
You may think that adding up the padding and border to have the true size of your box is difficult, and you might be right. As a result, CSS launched an additional box model a little later than a standard box model. Every width on the webpage is the visible width of the box, so the width of the content area is the width minus the border and padding width.

Example

The following is the result of using that CSS example as before (height = 150px, width = 350px).

Output:

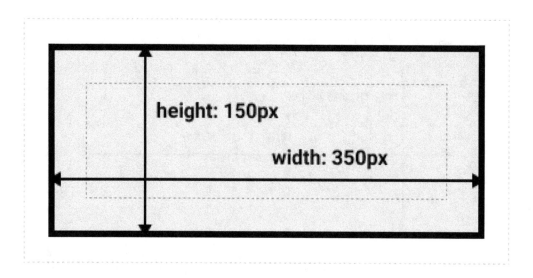

3.4 Why CSS Box Model Is Important?

You've dealt with the box model if you've ever been working on a web page layout and find yourself doing every kind of calculation to sort out how big or wide you should create things and yet have them act appropriately on the page. It's essential to comprehend how margins, borders, padding, and text all fit together to build the page's layout.

3.5 Summary of Box Model

- Boxes should be used to describe all the HTML elements present on the web page.
- The word "Box Model" in CSS defines the layout and design of a page.
- Box Model is made up of the following elements: margins, borders, padding, and the real content.
- We have the ability to modify the width and height of the elements (boxes).
- Box Model enables one to specify the amount of space between components/elements.

- We may use Box Model to insert borders across the elements.

Chapter 4: Positioning and Floating

A lack of comprehension of CSS's position, display, and float properties is among the most popular CSS issues that others are struggling with. Elements on the website will resize, rearrange and do all but what you're striving to do when you set out the designing for your website. In a frenzy of trial and error, you test any combination of various CSS properties on child and parent divs. Nothing seems to be running. You yell with frustration. There has to be a reason for the chaos. Positioning and floating make all of these easy for us.

4.1 Position

Position property defines how an object is placed on the web page or in relation to other items. Position's default value is static, which means that items displayed on the web page as same as they display on the document. The top, bottom, left, and right properties are then used to place the elements. These properties, though, position property has to be set first set in order to make these properties work. They often behave differently based on the value of the position.

It consists of five values. These are as under:

- Static
- Fixed
- Relative
- Absolute

Syntax

A single keyword, such as static, relative, fixed or absolute, is used to specify it.

Example

position: relative;

4.1.1 Types of Position

It consists of four types. These are as under:

- Static
- Fixed
- Relative
- Absolute

static

The static position is by default use for every element. The element is placed in accordance with the document's usual flow. The top, bottom, left, and right properties have little effect on static positioned components or elements.

Example

div.static {

  position: static;

  border: 3px solid #73AD21;

}

Output:

position: static;

An element with position: static; is not positioned in any special way; it is always positioned according to the normal flow of the page:

This div element has position: static;

fixed

It also excludes elements from the document's flow, just as it is done by absolute positioned components or elements. In reality, they behave almost identical; the only difference is that fixed-position components are often relative to the file or document and not with any specific parent; also, they are unchanged by scrolling. The values for right, top, left, and bottom decides it's final location.

A static element should not leave a blank space on the website where it will usually be located.

Example

```
div.fixed {
  position: fixed;
  bottom: 0;
  right: 0;
  width: 300px;
  border: 3px solid #73AD21;
}
```

Output:

position: fixed;

An element with position: fixed; is positioned relative to the viewport, which means it always stays in the same place even if the page is scrolled:

This div element has position: fixed;

relative

The element, such as static value, is placed according to the document's usual flow. However, right, left, bottom, top, and z-index can now work. The element's positional properties "push" it in that path from it's original location. Other content would not be resized to fit through the element's void.

Example

div.relative {

 position: relative;

 left: 30px;

 border: 3px solid #73AD21;

}

Output:

position: relative;

An element with position: relative; is positioned relative to its normal position:

This div element has position: relative;

absolute

When an element or a component that is completely positioned is removed from the flow, other components are placed as though they never existed. In page layout, no space is provided for the component. The position of the element with absolute position is proportional to the closest positioned ancestor.

When the absolute position element seems to have no position ancestors, it uses the document structure and scrolls with the page. Values of right, top, left, and bottom decides it's final location.

Example

div.relative {

position: relative;

width: 400px;

height: 200px;

border: 3px solid #73AD21;

```
  }

div.absolute {
 position: absolute;
 top: 80px;
right: 0;
width: 200px;
height: 100px;
border: 3px solid #73AD21;
 }
```

Output:

position: absolute;

An element with position: absolute; is positioned relative to the nearest positioned ancestor (instead of positioned relative to the viewport, like fixed):

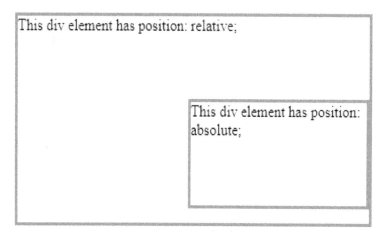

4.2 Floating

CSS's float property is used to position elements. We should look at the print design to grasp it's intent and origin. Images should be set on the page just like text wraps over them when required in a print design. This is referred to as "text wrap" in the industry. Here's an illustration of it.

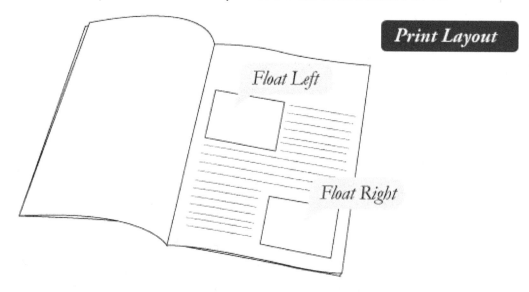

The text-holding boxes in the layout of the page's programs may be ordered to honor or ignore the text wrap. By skipping text wrap, the words would spill over the picture as though they weren't even there. That's the distinction between the image or picture being a portion of page flow or not becoming a portion of page flow. The two are very close in terms of web design.

Think about an inline variable nesting inside a <p>, such as <img>. When the float value is set to 'left,' the image will be on left side, and the text will be on the right side, wrapping to a complete line under where the image finishes. Setting the clear property on another component (as in <p> next to one floated <img>) prevents the image from floating to either or both sides. Without using tables, the float property of CSS enables a developer to use table-like columns inside the HTML layout. CSS designs will not be feasible without the CSS float attribute and would thus depend on absolute and relative positioning, which will be complicated and unmaintainable.

Note: Float property is ignored by the absolute positioned components(elements).

CSS Demo: float

float: none;

float: left;

float: right;

Syntax

- **Short-hand**

float: none|left|right|initial|inherit;

- **Long-hand**

float: left;

float: right;

float: none;

float: inherit;

float: initial;

Example

Let an image float to the right:

img {

float: right;

}

Output:

The float Property

In this example, the image will float to the right in the text, and the text in the paragraph will wrap around the image.

Lorem ipsum dolor sit amet, consectetur adipiscing elit. Phasellus imperdiet, nulla et dictum interdum, nisi lorem egestas odio, vitae scelerisque enim ligula venenatis dolor. Maecenas nisl est, ultrices nec congue eget, auctor vitae massa. Fusce luctus vestibulum augue ut aliquet. Mauris ante ligula, facilisis sed ornare eu, lobortis in odio. Praesent convallis urna a lacus interdum ut hendrerit risus congue. Nunc sagittis dictum nisi, sed ullamcorper ipsum dignissim ac. In at libero sed nunc venenatis imperdiet sed ornare turpis. Donec vitae dui eget tellus gravida venenatis. Integer fringilla congue eros non fermentum. Sed dapibus pulvinar nibh tempor porta. Cras ac leo purus. Mauris quis diam velit.

Values

There are four possible values for the float CSS property. These are as under:

- none
- left
- right
- inherit

none

It is not allowed for the element to float. For every element in the HTML page, the initial or default float value is none.

left

The element has to float to the left of the block in which it is contained.

right

The element has to float to the right of the block in which it is contained.

inherit

The float would be passed down from the parent element to the child element.

4.2.1 Clearing Floats

The CSS clear property, which allows you to "clear" floating components from the right or left side, or from both sides, of a component, is widely used to solve layout problems with floats.

Syntax

It has the following syntax:

clear: value;

Value

It's values are as under:

- left
- right
- both
- none
- inherit

left

In this value, the element has been pushed down to clear the left-floated components(elements)

Syntax

It's syntax is:

clear: left;

right

In this value, the element has been pushed down to clear the right-floated components(elements)

Syntax

It's syntax is:

clear: right;

both

The element is pushed down to clear both right and left floated components.

Syntax

It's syntax is:

clear: both;

none

To clear certain floated elements, the element would not be pushed down.

Syntax

It's syntax is:

clear: none;

inherit

The clear will be passed down from the parent element to the child element.

Syntax

It's syntax is:

clear: inherit;

Chapter 5: Display and Visibility

Now let's talk about some more CSS properties.

5.1 Display

Each website element is defined by the box that carries content and controls the number of spaces around it. We've learned how to place these boxes on the website, but there's always something we should do. The display property of CSS controls how a box displays on a page in relation to other components and also how the child elements of the box behave. To put it another way, it controls how the rectangular box of a website acts. The most strong and helpful property in CSS is the display property. This can be really helpful for designing websites that have a unique appearance but also adhering to web standards.

Syntax

display: value;

Example

Some uses of various display values are as under:

p.ex1 {display: none;}

p.ex2 {display: inline;}

p.ex3 {display: block;}

p.ex4 {display: inline-block;}

Output:

The display Property

display: none:

Lorem ipsum dolor sit amet, consectetur adipiscing elit. Etiam semper diam at erat pulvinar, at pulvinar felis blandit. Vestibulum volutpat tellus diam, consequat gravida libero rhoncus ut.

display: inline:

Lorem ipsum dolor sit amet, consectetur adipiscing elit. Etiam semper diam at erat pulvinar, at pulvinar felis blandit. HELLO WORLD! Vestibulum volutpat tellus diam, consequat gravida libero rhoncus ut.

display: block:

Lorem ipsum dolor sit amet, consectetur adipiscing elit. Etiam semper diam at erat pulvinar, at pulvinar felis blandit.

HELLO WORLD!

Vestibulum volutpat tellus diam, consequat gravida libero rhoncus ut.

Values

Some widely used display values are as under:

- block
- grid
- inline
- inline-block
- none
- flex

Brief description of these values are:

Block

This Element begins from the new line and occupies the whole width by default (if no width is specified). Other inline element or blocks can be present in it.

It's purpose is to display a the element into the block element. The default block elements include <p>, <div>, <ul>, <li>, <canvas> and <h1>-<h6>.

Example

```
span {
    display: block;
}
a {
    display: block;
}
```

Output:

Visit tutorialrepublic.com

This span element generates a block box.

grid

It displays the element as the block-level of a grid container. Display property will also set the grid layout at the start.

Syntax

```
body {
  display: grid;
}
```

inline

The element will begin anywhere on a line that already exists. They are unaffected by the height and width properties. Any element with the inline display attribute became the inline element. These elements can display on a similar line as <span> elements without breaking. The default inline elements include <span>, <input>, <button> and <img>.

inline-block

This is meant to display the element as the inline-level of the block container, but the width and height can be adapted. Since grid, table, and flex are block-level components, they can be applied with them.

none

It clears the page from the desired element and all of it's children. When an entity has none value, it generates no boxes whatsoever. And if the display property's value is set to anything except none, then the child elements will not create any boxes. As a result, corresponding elements act as though this component doesn't exist.

flex

In a flexbox layout, it's used to display the element like a block-level of a flex container.

5.2 Visibility

Visibility property determines if or not the element is evident without altering the page's layout; moreover, hidden elements consume the space in the website. In <table>, the property may also be used to hide columns or rows. Set a display property with none rather than using visibility to hide and remove an element from the page's layout.

Syntax

It's syntax can be declared by using two properties. These are:

- **Short-hand Property**

visibility: visible|hidden|collapse|initial|inherit;

- **Long-hand Property**

visibility: visible;

visibility: hidden;

visibility: collapse;

visibility: inherit;

Example

Make <h2> elements invisible:

```
h2 {
visibility: hidden;
}
```

Output:

This is a visible heading

Notice that the invisible heading still takes up space.

Values

It's values are as under:

- visible
- hidden
- collapse
- inherit

Brief description of these values are as under:

visible

It's the default value. Visible, as the name implies, makes the contents and it's box visible.

hidden

Even if an element is opaque, it still occupies space. If the element's descendants have visibility adjusted to visible, they will become visible. This is not the same as utilizing display: none, because hidden just hides elements visually. An element is indeed present and occupies space mostly on the website, but it is no longer visible.

collapse

Just table elements can use this property. Collapse eliminates a column or row from the table and has no effect on the layout. The column or row's space would be freed to accommodate other content. The collapse has the same effect as hidden when applied to other elements.

inherit

This is a default value. This essentially means that the element will inherit a value from it's parent, i.e., it will have similar visibility as it's parent.

Chapter 6: Background

It is the most effective and complicated property in CSS. CSS background property allows us to manage the dimensions and attributes of the images, allowing us to make images that are responsive to both smaller and wider screens. As a result, we're able to create more responsive websites. It is also a shorthand property, that means it lets you compose what otherwise would be multiply.

Example

Various background properties can be set in a single declaration such as:

```
body {
    background: #00ff00 url("smiley.gif") no-repeat fixed center;
}
```

Output:

This is some text

This is some text

This is some text

This is some text

This is some text

This is some text

This is some text

This is some text

This is some text

This is some text

This is some text

This is some text

This is some text

This is some text

Syntax

background: value;

Values

Some of it's commonly used values are:

- background-size
- auto-sizing
- background-color
- background-image
- background-position
- background-repeat
- background-attachment

background-size

A background image size is defined here.

Syntax

background-size: cover;

background-size can be used in three different ways:

   i.   use the Cover/Contain value

   ii.   set width and height of an image

   iii.   use auto

This property can be used to adjust the image's width and height.

Syntax

.container{

// here, we see width & height

  background-size : 200px   200px;

}

auto-sizing

The image would remain at it's initial size while this value is used. When the screen is resized, it won't change anything.

background-color

This property specifies the color of an element's background.

Syntax

.container{

background-color : blue;

}

background-image

One or more background images can be set using this property. Gradients and regular images are the two kinds of images that may be included using CSS.

Syntax

It's simple to use an image as a background like:

```
body {
  background: url(helloworld.jpg);
}
```

The url() attribute enables you to specify the path of a file to some image, which will be used as the element's background.

background-image can be used in two ways:

- By allocating the path of the image inside the directory.
- By giving the URL of an image.

background-position

It's purpose is to adjust the image's location on the window.

Syntax

```
html {
  background-position: 150px 10px;
}
```

Value

There are three kinds of values in it:

- Length values (for example, 100px 5px)
- Percentages (for example, 100% 5%)
- Keywords (for example, top right)

0 0 are it's default values. This positions the background picture in the container's top right corner.

background-repeat

It defines how the background pictures can be repeated.

Syntax

```
html {
  background-image: url(build.png);
```

```
    background-repeat: repeat-x;
}
```

Value

It consists of six values. Which are as under:

- repeat
- no-repeat
- repeat-x
- repeat-y
- round
- space

background-attachment

It determines whether the document's background is scrolling with it or stays rooted in the display region.

Syntax

```
.container{
background-attachment: scroll;
}
```

This property can be used to adjust the image's height and width.

Value

It consists of three values:

- scroll
- fixed
- local

Chapter 7: Text and Font

CSS's font and text properties control how single characters in a line or word of text appear.

7.1 Text

The text property in CSS is applied to style and format text.

The following properties are used in this property:

- Text-color
- Word spacing
- Letter spacing
- Text-alignment
- Text-decoration
- Line height

7.1.1 Text color

This property is applied to add the text's color.

The name "blue", the hex value "#ff0010" or the RGB value "rgb(190,0,5) can all be used to change the color of the text.

Syntax

body

{

color:color name;

}

Example

h1 {

color: green;

}

7.1.2 Word spacing

The space present in between words of a sentence is described by word spacing. It allows negative values; the value should be in duration format.

Syntax

body

{

word-spacing:size;

}

Examples

P.note { word-spacing: -0.3em }

P EM { word-spacing: 0.6em }

7.1.3 Letter spacing

It is used to determine the amount of space within text characters. Length format must be used for the value. It also allows negative values. A value of 0 disables justification.

Syntax

body

{

letter-spacing:size;

}

Examples

P.note { letter-spacing: -0.1em }

H1 { letter-spacing: 0.1em }

7.1.4 Text-alignment

The use of this property is to adjust the text's horizontal alignment. The text may also be aligned to the right, left, justified or centered.

Syntax

body

```
{
   text-align:alignment type;
   }
```

Example

P.newspaper { text-align: justify }

H1{ text-align: center }

7.1.5 text-decoration
The use of this property is to remove or add decorations from a piece of text.

Text may be none, line-through, overline or underlined.

Syntax

body

```
{
text-decoration:decoration type;
}
```

Example

If you don't want to underline the link, then use this;

A:link, A:visited, A:active { text-decoration: none }

7.1.6 line-height
This property sets the line space. Whenever the value is an integer or a number, multiply the font size of the element by it to get a line-height. The percentage value is proportional to the font size of the element. It doesn't allow negative values. Also, with the font size, line height can also be specified with in font property.

Syntax

body

```
{
line-height:size;
}
```

Example

It can be used to add double space to the text. Such as:

P { line-height: 200% }

7.2 Font Property

It is again a shorthand property. Any single value which is not defined is reset to it's initial value, much as any other shorthand property.

Syntax

font: font-style font-weight font-size   font-family|caption|icon|menu|message-box|small-caption|status-bar|initial|inherit;

Example

By using shorthand declaration, you can set certain font properties:

p.a {

font: 15px Arial, sans-serif;

}

p.b {

 font: italic small-caps bold 12px/30px Georgia, serif;

}

Output:

The font Property

This is a paragraph. The font size is set to 15 pixels, and the font family is Arial.

This is a paragraph. The font is set to italic and bold, with small-caps (all lowercase letters are converted to uppercase). The font size is set to 12 pixels, the line height is set to 30 pixels, and the font family is Georgia.

Values

Some of it's values are:

- font-style
- font-weight
- font-size
- font-family

font-style

This property specifies if a font must be styled by it's italic, oblique or normal face. "Normal" is the default value for this property.

Syntax

It's syntax are as under:

- font-style: normal;
- font-style: italic;
- font-style: oblique;
- font-style: inherit;

font-weight

The thickness or font-weight is defined by this property. "Normal" is the default value of this property. The available weights are determined by the font-family, which is currently identified.

Syntax

Some of it's syntaxes are:

- font-weight: normal;
- font-weight: bold;
- font-weight: lighter;
- font-weight: bolder;

font-size

It specifies the line height and font size are specified. "Natural" is again the default value of this property.

Syntax

Some of it's syntaxes are:

- font-size: small;
- font-size: medium;
- font-size: large;
- font-size: smaller;
- font-size: larger;
- font-size: 12px;
- font-size: 80%;

font-family

It defines the font to be used on the element. It defines a collection of fonts in order of preference, from highest to lowest. The browser determines the default value of the font-family. Since there's no assurance that any particular font would be available, so you have to always add at least a single common family name inside a font-family list. This allows the browser to choose an appropriate fallback font whenever it is required.

Syntax

Some of it's syntaxes are:

- font-family: serif;
- font-family: sans-serif;
- font-family: monospace;
- font-family: cursive;
- font-family: inherit;
- font-family: initial;

Chapter 8: List, links and Navigation bars

Now, let's learn about the list, links and navigation bars.

8.1 Lists

Lists are the common thing in daily life. To-do lists help you figure out what has to be done. Instructions and ingredients are both listed in the recipes. It is indeed easy to see why they're so famous online, with such a list for almost everything. Lists are extremely useful for conveying a series of bullet or numbered points. It enables you to create a list of items for unordered or ordered lists by using separate list object markings. Colors may be added to the background of the lists, and it's list elements. You can also add an image to the list object marker.

8.1.1 List types
There are three types of lists. These are as under:

- **Unordered list**

Unordered lists are used to organize a group of similar items that aren't arranged in any specific order.

- **Ordered list**

Ordered lists are used to organize a group of similar items into a specific order.

- **Description list**

Description lists are used to visualize value or name pairs like definitions and terms.

8.1.2 List style property
Lists can be controlled by using the four Cascading Style Sheets properties that are mentioned below:

- list-style
- list-style-type

- list-style-image
- list-style-position

These are briefly explained below:

- **list-style**

It is the shorthand property. These properties could emerge in any sequence. It sets all of the properties of the list in a single declaration.

Example

ul {

list-style: square inside url("sqpurple.gif");

}

Output:

CSS Lists

The list-style property is a shorthand property, which is used to set all the list properties in one declaration.

- Coffee
- Tea
- Coca Cola

Values

While using a shorthand property, it's values are mentioned in the following order:

list-style-type

list-style-position

list-style-image

If either of the mentioned property values is missing, then it's default value, if any, will be used.

- **list-style-type**

It helps you to manage the marker's appearance or shape. The marker's color is much like the calculated color of an element to which it applies. Furthermore, since as it is an inherited property, it could be applied to every list item by setting it on the parent element.

Example

Set some different list styles:

ul.a {list-style-type: circle;}

ul.b {list-style-type: square;}

ol.c {list-style-type: upper-roman;}

ol.d {list-style-type: lower-alpha;}

Output:

The list-style-type Property

Example of unordered lists:

- Coffee
- Tea
- Coca Cola

- Coffee
- Tea
- Coca Cola

Example of ordered lists:

I. Coffee
II. Tea
III. Coca Cola

a. Coffee
b. Tea
c. Coca Cola

Syntax

list-style-type: value;

Values

A few of them are as under:

disc

- It is a default value

- It is a completely filled circle

circle

- It's an empty circle

square

- It's a completely filled square

decimal

1. These are decimal numbers
2. It begins with 1

lower-roman

i. These are lowercase roman numbers

ii. For example, i, ii, iii, iv, v...

upper-roman

I. These are uppercase roman numbers

II. For example, I, II, III, IV, V...

- **list-style-image**

You may use it to classify an image to apply a customized bullet style. It is not possible to resize the image. It's syntax is identical to that property of the background-image, with the URL preceding the property value and the URL enclosed in brackets. If it is left blank, then none is set by default, which means default bullets are used. Instead of a number or bullet point, it defines an image to set as a marker.

Syntax

list-style-image: value;

Values

It's values are as follow:

none

This property determines that an image can not be used as a list marker. It is used as a default value.

initial

It sets the default value of the property.

url

It is the direction of the image's location, which is used as a marker.

inherit

The value of the element is inherited by their parent element.

Example

Below, we'll go through this property and will look at an example about how to apply it in CSS.

Using List Items

You may also apply this property to a list item directly, as given here:

li { list-style-image: url("/images/symbol.gif"); }

This will also lead to the following list items emerging (irrespective of if a list item is ordered (sorted) or unordered):

- TechOnTheNet.com
- CheckYourMath.com
- BigActivities.com

In this example, the circle from the rear of every list item in a <ul> tag would be exchanged with the blue.gif image.

- **list-style-position**

This property specifies if the marker must be placed within or outside the bullet-point box. It determines if a large point which wraps to the second line can coincide with it's first line or begin underneath the marker's start.

Syntax

It's syntax is as under:

Values

It consists of three values. These are as under:

- Outside
- inside
- inherit

outside

Marker box should be on the outside of the main block box. It is set by default.

Syntax

ul { list-style-position: outside; }

inside

Marker box should be located within the main block box.

Syntax

ul { list-style-position: inside; }

inherit

List-style-position of an element is inherited from it's own parent element.

Syntax:

ol { list-style-position: inherit; }

8.2 Links

A link is an attachment between two or more web pages. CSS properties may be applied to style attachments in a variety of ways. Buttons or boxes may also be applied to style CSS links.

8.2.1 The Link's States

Links could exist in various states

The following are the four states of the links:

a:link

It is a regular link that hasn't been visited.

Syntax

```
a:link {
    color:color_name;
}
```

a:hover

It's a link when the mouse floats over it.

Syntax

```
a:hover {
    color:color_name;
}
```

a:visited

It is the link that a user has visited at-least once.

Syntax

```
a:visited {
    color:color_name;
}
```

a:active

It is a recently clicked link.

Syntax

a:active {

   color:color_name;

}

Links defaults values:

- All links created by default are underlined.

- The hand icon appears when the mouse is floated over a link.

- Links that haven't been accessed are blue in color.

- Purple colored links are those who have been visited.

- Active links are represented by red color.

- A focused link is surrounded by an outline.

8.2.2 Links Properties
The following are some basic CSS properties for the links:

- text-decoration

- color

- background-color

- font-family

text-decoration

The purpose of this property is to remove or add underlines from the link.

Syntax

```
a {
    text-decoration: none;
}
```

color

The color of the link text can be changed by using it.

Syntax

```
a {
    color: color_name;
}
```

background-color

It sets the color of the link's background.

Syntax

```
a {
    background-color: color_name;
}
```

font-family

Using this property, you may modify a font type of the link.

Syntax:

```
a {
    font-family: "family name";
}
```

8.3 Navigation Bar

As a foundation, a navigation bar requires standard HTML. A collection of links which lead to various pages of the website is referred to as a navigation bar in CSS. Horizontal or vertical navigation bars are available.

By two elements, HTML forms the framework of a navigation bar. These are as under:

- <ul>
- <li>

Example 1

```
<ul>
  <li><a href="default.asp">Home</a></li>
  <li><a href="news.asp">News</a></li>
  <li><a href="contact.asp">Contact</a></li>
  <li><a href="about.asp">About</a></li>
</ul>
```

Output:

- Home
- News
- Contact
- About

Note: We use href="#" for test links. In a real web site this would be URLs.

Now exclude the bullets, as well as the padding and margins from a list:

Example 2

```
ul {
list-style-type: none;
margin: 0;
padding: 0;
}
```

Output:

In this example, we remove the bullets from the list, and its default padding and margin.

Home
News
Contact
About

It's essential to disable the default navigation bar settings of the browser.

Example explained

list-style-type:

Bullets are removed when none value is applied to the navigation bars.

margin: 0; and padding: 0;

It removes the existing or default spacing settings of the browser

Both horizontal and vertical navigation bars have these properties. The coding in the previous example is common for both horizontal and vertical navigation bars.

Chapter 9: Tables

In HTML, a <table> is used to view tabular data. It's a means of describing and displaying data that can be useful in spreadsheet applications. Or a nutshell, there are rows and columns.

Example

Below is a quick example of the tabular data:

```
<table>
  <tr>
    <th>Name</th>
    <th>ID</th>
    <th>Favorite Color</th>
  </tr>
  <tr>
    <td>Jim</td>
    <td>00001</td>
    <td>Blue</td>
  </tr>
  <tr>
    <td>Sue</td>
    <td>00002</td>
    <td>Red</td>
  </tr>
  <tr>
    <td>Barb</td>
    <td>00003</td>
    <td>Green</td>
  </tr>
```

```
</table>
```

Output:

Name	ID	Favorite Color
Jim	00001	Blue
Sue	00002	Red
Barb	00003	Green

9.1 Table Borders

Border property of CSS is used to define table borders.

For the <table>, <td>, and <th> components, the following example defines the black border:

Example

```
table, th, td {
  border: 1px solid black;
}
```

Output:

Add a border to a table:

Firstname	Lastname
Peter	Griffin
Lois	Griffin

9.2 Table Padding

Use this property upon on <td> and th> elements to manage the space within the content and the border in the table.

Example

```
th, td {
 padding: 15px;
 text-align: left;
}
```

Output:

The padding Property

This property adds space between the border and the content in a table.

Firstname	Lastname	Savings
Peter	Griffin	$100
Lois	Griffin	$150
Joe	Swanson	$300
Cleveland	Brown	$250

9.3 Table Alignment

There are two types of table alignments. These are:

- Horizontal alignment
- Vertical alignment

Now let's discuss them in detail:

9.3.1 Horizontal Alignment

This property specifies a horizontal alignment of the material in <td> or <th> (such as right, left, or centre). The composition of the <th> elements is center-aligned by default, while the composition of <td> elements is left-aligned. Using text-align: center; to align the material or content of the <td> component(element).

Example 1

```
td {
text-align: center;
}
```

Output:

The text-align Property

This property sets the horizontal alignment (like left, right, or center) of the content in th or td.

Firstname	Lastname	Savings
Peter	Griffin	$100
Lois	Griffin	$150
Joe	Swanson	$300
Cleveland	Brown	$250

For left-aligning a content, use text-align: left property; to push the alignment of the <th> elements so that it can be left-aligned.

Example 2

```
th {
text-align: left;
}
```
Output:

The text-align Property

This property sets the horizontal alignment (like left, right, or center) of the content in th or td.

Firstname	Lastname	Savings
Peter	Griffin	$100
Lois	Griffin	$150
Joe	Swanson	$300
Cleveland	Brown	$250

9.3.2 Vertical Alignment

Vertical-align property determines how the content in <td> or <th> is aligned vertically (such as bottom, middle or top). Vertical alignment is set to middle by default (for both <td> and <th> elements) of content that is present in the table.

Example:

td {

height: 50px;

vertical-align: bottom;

}

Output:

The vertical-align Property

This property sets the vertical alignment (like top, bottom, or middle) of the content in th or td.

Firstname	Lastname	Savings
Peter	Griffin	$100
Lois	Griffin	$150
Joe	Swanson	$300
Cleveland	Brown	$250

9.4 Table Width and Height

The height and width properties describe the height and height of the table. Width of a table is set to 100%, as well as height of <th> elements is set to 70px in the example given below:

Example 1

```
table {
  width: 100%;
}


th {
  height: 70px;
}
```


Output:

The width and height Properties

Set the width of the table, and the height of the table header row:

Firstname	Lastname	Savings
Peter	Griffin	$100
Lois	Griffin	$150
Joe	Swanson	$300
Cleveland	Brown	$250

Using width: 50%, to make a table which just covers half of the page in the following example.

Example 2

```
table {
  width: 50%;
}


th {
```

```
  height: 70px;
}
```

Output:

The width and height Properties

Set the width of the table, and the height of the table header row:

Firstname	Lastname	Savings
Peter	Griffin	$100
Lois	Griffin	$150
Joe	Swanson	$300
Cleveland	Brown	$250

Conclusion

HyperText Markup Language and Cascading Style Sheets are both used to create a website or web page. CSS, on the other hand, is trying to replace HTML because it has more flexibility and features. Consider CSS to be the color of the paint, window designs, and landscaping that falls after the base, doors, partitions, and girders that protect the website. You won't get far without laying the foundation, but when you do, then you would like to add some design. Cascading Style Sheets are the key to bringing out your inner designer. Who'd have guessed that HTML and CSS are such large subjects? If you came this far, you're on your road to mastering the front end production of a website. You can be even more at ease analysing and breaking the structure of the website into it's individual components and thereafter coding them in CSS. You now have the tools you need to define and implement an effective visual interface. You do have a lot of room to develop your skills and your understanding of best practices, so don't quit practicing and learning, yet you have all you need to create stunning websites with the help of Cascading Style Sheets.

In conclusion, all we can say is that the Cascading Style Sheets helps you customize your web page or website. It makes your web page look presentable to the users, and it also attracts new users by it's look and feel. It makes your web page look different from other web pages and makes it user friendly. It is easier than other languages because it lessens the amount of coding to enhance it's website's look because a single line of code can be used to change the whole or part of the website at once when required. It also has some shorthand properties, which are really helpful to shorten the code, and it saves a lot of web designers time and effort. As it helps to style text, fonts and coloring of a website, it also helps us to position, float, set backgrounds, style different types of lists, navigation bars and tables.